Billy Humphrey is a   ity,
authority, and pioneeri   to
insightful revelation of (ok
is both inspiring and pr   ne
reader with the motivatic _ ...uy pursue God and to
joyfully line one's life up with the truth!

—ANDY BYRD
YWAM, University of the Nations, Kona, Hawaii
Director, Fire and Fragrance
Coauthor, *Fire and Fragrance* and *Culture of Revival*

Billy Humphrey is a man gripped with a vision of the knowledge of God and seeing that knowledge fleshed out in his life, his family, and his ministry. I've known Billy and his family in a deeply personal way over the last ten years, and in that time I've witnessed a man who has been consumed with the same vision that possessed the apostle Paul: "The excellence of the knowledge of Christ Jesus." I believe that the loss of the majesty and glory of Jesus Christ has resulted in a thousand other evils that have destroyed Christian marriages, families, and ministries. Billy, in such a clear and convicting manner, gives us the high vision and then walks us through God's vision for marriage, family, finances, and life. This book called me higher in so many areas, and I'm convinced that it will do the same for you.

—COREY RUSSELL
Senior leader, International House of Prayer–Kansas City
Author, *Glory Within* and *Ancient Paths*

Any search of the unsearchable and pursuit of knowing the unknowable is an incredibly daunting task. Yet when we start the pursuit of the One we should fear the most, and discover He is the One who loves us the most, it is only the beginning to the adventure of a lifetime. My friend Billy Humphrey shares what God has revealed about Himself to him in the pages of this book. Written in a most creative way, with great depth, yet profoundly simple, Billy has put together through years of study, prayer, and time with the Father a book that not only sets you aflame but also will keep the fire of love burning on the altar of your heart. This book will put the "why" behind the "what" of God in our creation roles and is written by someone who knows God and has been willing to wrestle with Him over the hard questions in life. A must-read!

—WILL FORD III
Author, *History Makers* and
Created for Influence
www.willfordministries.com

Billy Humphrey's passion for Christ is contagious! The nuggets of insight that are only cultivated from a lifelong pursuit of His presence are beautifully communicated in a manner that will ignite your heart and have you running to your secret place eager to know Christ more intimately! A must-read for all who yearn to know Christ in His fullness and love!

—RICHARD CRISCO
Senior pastor, Rochester First Assembly of God
Rochester, MI

TO KNOW HIM

BILLY HUMPHREY

PASSIO

Most CHARISMA HOUSE BOOK GROUP products are available at special quantity discounts for bulk purchase for sales promotions, premiums, fund-raising, and educational needs. For details, write Charisma House Book Group, 600 Rinehart Road, Lake Mary, Florida 32746, or telephone (407) 333-0600.

TO KNOW HIM by Billy Humphrey
Published by Passio
Charisma Media/Charisma House Book Group
600 Rinehart Road
Lake Mary, Florida 32746
www.charismahouse.com

Unless otherwise noted, all Scripture quotations are from the New King James Version of the Bible. Copyright © 1979, 1980, 1982 by Thomas Nelson, Inc., publishers. Used by permission.

Scripture quotations marked NIV are from the Holy Bible, New International Version. Copyright © 1973, 1978, 1984, International Bible Society. Used by permission.

Scripture quotations marked NAS are from the New American Standard Bible, copyright © 1960, 1962, 1963, 1968, 1971, 1972, 1973, 1975, 1977, 1995 by The Lockman Foundation. Used by permission. (www.Lockman.org)

Cover design by Justin Evans and Lisa Rae Cox
Design Director: Bill Johnson

Visit the author's website at www.ihop-atlanta.com and on
Twitter, @BillyHumphrey1.

Library of Congress Control Number: 2013903002
International Standard Book Number: 978-1-62136-207-4
E-book ISBN: 978-1-62136-208-1

While the author has made every effort to provide accurate
telephone numbers and Internet addresses at the time of
publication, neither the publisher nor the author assumes
any responsibility for errors or for changes that occur after
publication.

First edition

13 14 15 16 17 — 987654321
Printed in the United States of America

To all those who desire to know God and proclaim Him as He is, I pray this book compels you into a pursuit that grants you a depth of understanding in the knowledge of God. You are the greatest hope for the earth in this hour.

CONTENTS

ACKNOWLEDGMENTS

I WANT TO THANK Wesley Huth for his incredible input and suggestions for this book. Wesley, your honesty and objectivity have helped me stretch and grow as a writer. You are a good friend and a trusted comrade.

I want to thank Jamie Burns-Pridgen for reading and rereading so many portions of the original manuscript of this book and offering constructive and helpful suggestions. Thanks for always spurring me on.

I want to thank Steven Ugan for his clear teachings on the knowledge of God in finances. Your insights have greatly helped to form my ideas on this most important topic. You're a faithful colleague and friend.

I appreciate my friend Corey Russell for being the first one to challenge me in the pursuit of the knowledge of God. Corey, your passion and hunger for God pricked my heart and helped launch me into this pursuit.

I appreciate Gary Thomas for his insightful input and forthright feedback. Your honesty and encouragement have helped me and stretched me. Your integrity is rare.

I am grateful for Mike Bickle and his example as a standard-bearer who has fought for depth in the knowledge of God and encouraged me to do the same. Mike, your example is compelling.

BILLY HUMPHREY'S CANDID boldness from the outset of this book is about to refresh you. I mean, how many authors are willing to begin their book by saying they know practically nothing about the topic on which they are about to write?

Billy speaks of an encounter in which he was suddenly made aware of how little he knew God. I had an experience of my own that parallels Billy's to a certain extent. I had come to a place in my journey with God where I had hit a wall, so to speak. All I knew to do was say to the Lord: "Jesus, I am going to set aside everything that I *think* I know about You and come to Your words, life, and teachings as though I'm reading them for the first time. I'm asking You to show me who You really are." With that prayer, I went on a focused study of the life of Christ in the Gospels. I had a red-letter Bible, in which Jesus's words were printed in red ink, so if it was red, I read it.

I was not prepared for what followed. Over and again I was impacted with how different Jesus was from the Jesus I had formulated in my mind. Maybe I had an image of Jesus that was merely the best version of myself. I don't know. I *do* know that I found myself repeatedly saying to myself, "He is nothing like me!"

Rather than being repelled or put off by what I was discovering about Jesus, I found myself falling in love with Him all over again.

Jesus is a unique person. (See Job 23:13.) There is no one else in the universe like Him. The greatest mistake you can make is to think you know who He is even before you've spent time with Him. He thinks differently from you. His values and priorities will catch you off guard. The more you come to know Him, the more you'll be surprised at the things that really bother Him and the things He easily dismisses. He is a unique personality, and there's only one way to get to know Him. It's the same way you get to know anybody: you have to spend time with Him.

Get ready—this book is catalytic. It's not the kind of book you can easily dismiss without grappling over personal change.

We might be tempted to think the knowledge of God is esoteric or impractical, but Billy Humphrey quickly brings us into reality. Knowing God is one of the most practical pursuits of the Christian life, because it's the knowledge of God that produces the most profound change in our lives. And when we're different at the core of our being, we act and respond differently in every arena of life.

This book is an abrupt wake-up call, but it's more than that. It's written to awaken within our hearts an insatiable hunger for the greatest thing the human heart can pursue. Will you join us in this ultimate quest—the knowledge of God?

—Bob Sorge
Kansas City, MO

WHEN GOD IS the subject of any investigation, an honest examiner will uncover more questions than answers. This book is likely to do just that. My intention isn't to drum up so many uncertainties that you're left bewildered. My intention is to offer you new views of God that will spur your heart into deeper and deeper inquiry.

Who is God? It's a question people have asked since the onset of Creation. At times God has answered it by making Himself known in unmistakable ways, by appearing and presenting Himself with such clarity that even the dimmest among us could not have missed His revealing. At other times God has veiled Himself from us, leaving only hints of His presence embroidered in the fabric of the living world. In these seasons He has not left us without a witness. He has neatly woven depictions of Himself throughout the channels of creation like the signature of a master artisan hardly detectable on a canvas. The very creation itself declares God; the heavens and the earth continually array Him. And more than the subtle inscription of God in nature, He has also crafted the operations of life to testify to Himself.

Indeed, all of life's institutions disclose God's handiwork because they reveal His nature.

God is truly mysterious—an expedition for an explorer, a journey for a discoverer, the pinnacle of all possible treasures to be prospected by man. It is our glory to search Him out.

The most magnificent journey of my life has been to seek for the knowledge of God. No ministry endeavor or human undertaking even compares to the magnificence of this quest. In fact, this quest is the entirety of every life's journey.

When we imagine life to be primarily about us, as if we are the center around which everything else orbits, we have completely missed God's design. He didn't create life's institutions to circle *our* world, responding to *our* whims, declaring truths about *us*. Rather, every one of life's relationships and institutions declare *Him*. They forever orbit the One who created it all, continually testifying to His beauty, emotions, character, and nature.

It is a disastrous error to imagine the world revolves around humanity. Though we may not admit this is our belief, often our approach states otherwise. We work and strain to better ourselves using chiefly human means. Slogans such as "Be all that you can be," "Five steps to success," and "Build a better you" fill our minds and shape our culture. From this human-centered focus we instruct others how to become better husbands, wives, employees, and people.

What if God isn't interested in making a better you? What if He isn't interested in making your life better or easier at all? That may sound like heresy to some because of the amount of teaching that affirms the contrary. But the testimony of Scripture offers a different view of God's purposes and a different paradigm for His blessing.

For instance, Jesus said, "Blessed are those who are persecuted...for theirs is the kingdom of heaven" (Matt. 5:8, NIV). That's quite a different idea of blessing than what is commonly espoused in pop-culture Christianity. I believe God wants to bless His people, but I don't believe ease and comfort are the sole—or even primary—means by which He blesses us. Our view of this kind of blessing often causes us to go about life with a primarily human focus. With this view we never dig even an inch deeper to find out if there's more to it than what might make us happier or more comfortable.

I propose that life is not primarily about us; it's primarily about God. All of life is about Him. All relationships, as well as the institutions of family, work, finance, and ministry are about God. They're designed by God to declare Himself to us.

God has placed us in the arena of life with a loaded set of circumstances, all of which continually beckon to us of Himself. Like walking through an art gallery, admiring the handiwork of the masters displayed on pedestals and in portraits, all the channels of life declare the knowledge and nature of God. He made everything to tell us about Himself.

This brings us back to life's purpose. If it's not about our betterment, what's it about? Simply: God. Life is about God. All of life's interactions are about Him. He is forever telling us of Himself through each institution. And His primary interest in all of it is for us to come to know Him.

Life doesn't orbit around us. It revolves around Him. Life is not about us becoming better. It's about us coming to know God. And in the knowledge of God, we find blessing, meaning, and understanding (2 Pet. 1:3). Through encountering and knowing God, each one of life's transactions becomes meaningful.

I submit that the only possible way to have a better life is to know the One who created the fabric of life to begin with. The book you're holding invites you to take a journey into the knowledge of God. And hopefully you will come to view and experience life the way He designed it to be viewed and experienced. Come with me as we forge ahead on this most challenging—yet exhilarating—expedition in all creation.

PART I

FOUNDATIONS

CHAPTER 1

WHO ARE YOU, LORD?

I THOUGHT I KNEW Him.

However, if I'm completely honest, I really don't. He's so much different than I imagined.

That's right, I'm confessing to you that I don't know God. Not really. Not deeply. Not in the way my heart craves.

I'm not saying I've never met Him or that I'm not saved. I'm saying that what I imagined I knew of God was thin and pale compared to what I've found out is available. I have found out that knowing God is a process that happens by degrees. A journey that takes an eternity. Most often when we believe we've come to know Him, it's an indicator of our lack, not our attainment.

After years of ministry I had grown comfortable in my relationship with God. I preached without preparing, counseled without consulting Him, and taught without talking to Him. In my mind those were signs of spiritual maturity—signs that I was intimately familiar with God. I now recognize those as the warning signs of an unhealthy ministry and traits of a heart that is distant from God. I thought I was intimate with Him like a close friend, one you're so aware of that you perceive what they feel even before they speak. To my shock and by His mercy, this One I thought I knew threw back the curtain to reveal Himself to me, and as my eyes focused, before me stood a stranger. He was completely different than what I imagined, as different as a dream is from reality.

I'm sure the question on your mind is, "Why are you writing a book about knowing God if you don't know Him yourself?" Because I'm convinced that none of us truly know Him—not compared to how much of Him there is to know. And definitely not compared to how much we *think* we know Him. I resonate deeply with Elihu's words: "Behold, God is great, and we do not know Him" (Job 36:26). With the exact same tone David adds, "His greatness is unsearchable" (Ps. 145:3), and Paul exults, "His ways [are] past finding out" (Rom. 11:33). If these biblical heroes confessed that God was beyond their knowledge, where does that leave you and me? Their explanations are not designed to discourage us from pursuing God, but rather they are admonitions alerting us to the size of our subject. When we're talking about knowing God—the God who created the universe, the God who Himself has no beginning or end—we have to be honest with ourselves about how much we *don't* know Him before we can dive into a study of knowing Him.

It's human nature to believe we understand things familiar to us. We lock into truths we think we know and become inflexible, no longer considering the alternative. Maybe it's our dullness or maybe it's our pride, but we don't tend to like new ideas that correct mistaken concepts we've believed. And to some extent, rightly so. It can be downright awkward and embarrassing to admit our lack of understanding. The departure from "what we know" into "what we've found out" feels unstable. Any time we leave the familiar for something new, we feel the clumsy uncertainty that comes with discovery. Like stepping into the sunlight after a day indoors, the moments it takes to adjust can be fairly unpleasant. But oh, the exhilaration that light brings! Light illuminates. Light clarifies. Light brings life. The humiliation of recognizing our dimness is nothing compared to the beauty and blessing of revealing light.

I know this awkward journey of discovery firsthand. There have been many moments God has revealed to me that things I believed about Him—even truths I held dear—were completely wrong. At other times He has revealed Himself to me in ways I had never before considered, opening up a flood of revelation I didn't know existed. Over the last decade, through these always-wonderful-but-sometimes-unpleasant moments of revelation, God has reinvented so much of my image of Him. I want to share some of my journey with you, in the hopes that it will open you up to new possibilities in your relationship with God and spur you into new insights about God's true purpose for our lives.

So let me tell you the beginning of my story.

In 2003 I was a youth pastor at a thriving local church in Atlanta, Georgia. I had worked feverishly for thirteen years to grow the ministry and reach as many people as possible. In the process I learned much about leadership and church growth. Our youth ministry blossomed to three hundred fifty in weekly attendance. I led a team of five staff members, twenty full-time interns, and seventy-five volunteer workers. The ministry was larger than 90 percent of the churches in America.

These accomplishments gave me the false sense that I truly knew the Lord. How wrong I was! In a very simple but most unexpected way I was confronted with my lack of knowledge.

Here's how that happened. After transitioning our

family and ministry to Kansas City, Missouri, to work at the International House of Prayer, I was invited to be part of a Bible study made up of mostly twenty-five-year-olds. Mike Bickle, the director of the house of prayer, was the leader of the study, and the attendees were some of his staff. I assumed that among this group I was a senior believer because I was a decade older than most of them. I figured these young people were novices in the faith, since many were young enough to have been in my youth group.

I was excited about the Bible study, anticipating the new opportunities I would have to learn with Mike, make new relationships, and mentor some of the younger believers. Within a few minutes of the very first meeting my wake-up call came. To my surprise I was completely out of my league. One by one my new friends began to effortlessly discuss biblical truths. I remember they discussed the role of Old Testament prophets as mouthpieces for the Lord and the necessity of preachers today to be vessels who could clearly and powerfully expound truths from the depths of the heart of God. They quoted from Amos, Micah, Isaiah, and Zechariah, books totally unfamiliar to me. They not only knew a lot of verses, but they also spoke with a depth of revelation I had never seen before. Much of what they discussed were concepts I'd never even considered.

I was blown away. To these young people the knowledge of God wasn't a bunch of head knowledge or a mere parroting of Scriptures. Revelation poured from their hearts with authority. It was evident they knew God in a way I didn't. It left me dumbfounded.

Unfortunately pride doesn't die easily. As I clamored internally, I sought to offer something meaningful to the conversation. I bumbled and stumbled and interjected a few thoughts about lions as pictures of prophets that awkwardly halted the study, causing Mike to have to jump-start the discussion to get it rolling again. The more I spoke, the more trivial I knew I sounded. I felt embarrassed and exposed. Though I had read the Bible from cover to cover several times, though I had delivered hundreds of sermons to literally thousands of people, and though I had built a thriving ministry over the course of many years, in just one moment on that Sunday afternoon I came face-to-face with the fact that my understanding of God's Word was very limited and my knowledge of God was shallow.

What was their secret? How had they come to such depth in God at such a young age? Several had been saved less time than I'd been in ministry!

I came to learn they all had one thing in common. Over the course of several years each of them had spent hours upon hours studying the Scriptures, fasting and praying, making the primary pursuit of their lives to know God.

Thankfully, being the youngest of three brothers, I've been conditioned not to accept defeat easily. When faced with a challenge, I typically respond with a desire to fight—a benefit of surviving many wrestling bouts where I was outmanned. And so, though I was painfully aware of my lack of the knowledge of God, my heart was ignited with a hunger to aggressively pursue knowing Him. I knew I was saved, and I loved the Lord, but it was evident I didn't truly *know* Him—not in the way those young believers did. I realized through their example that there's far more of God available than I imagined. My heart craved to know Him more deeply, and I was compelled to begin a journey into the knowledge of God that continues to this day.

Truth and Deception

Deception is sneaky. It's hard to detect. It's been said deception is difficult to deal with because it's so deceiving. No one who is deceived believes they are deceived, and therein lies the problem. Deception is present wherever truth is absent. So to one degree or another everyone is at least a little bit deceived. The one who thinks he is not deceived is likely the most deceived of the bunch!

Throughout our lives we have the continual opportunity to move from what is false to what is true, out of deception into verity. But discovering new truths presents us with a dilemma. Do we hold tight to what we think we already know, or do we abandon the familiar for the uncharted territory of revelation? The dilemma of discovery deepens the more sure we are about what we think we know. And the more sure we are about something, the more thrown off we are when we find out that what we thought we knew was, in fact, completely wrong. In other words, the journey into light is more challenging the more committed we are to our wrong ideas. If we embrace the light, the possibilities for growth are vast. But if, when light reveals the truth, we decide that our eyes are tricking us, that things are not really as they appear, we encase ourselves in a self-made prison of delusion. Oh yes, the prison is comfortable—only because it's familiar—but in the end, if we don't exit, we will remain bound, foreigners from freedom.

Throughout the Scriptures we find many examples of those who encountered God and were shocked by the light of revelation. God commissioned Noah to build an ark. He summoned Abraham to a strange land. He wrestled with Jacob and changed his name. He sent Joseph to prison on his way to the palace. He spoke to Moses at the burning bush. These are but a few examples of those who encountered God and found out He was altogether different than they expected.

Perhaps the greatest biblical example is the apostle Paul. Let's take a look at Paul's journey into the knowledge of God.

Paul's Example

Paul possessed an exemplary résumé. Born a Roman citizen, he was Jewish by heritage and educated under one of the most prestigious Jewish rabbis, Gamaliel. Paul's own words tell us more of his story: "Though I also might have confidence in the flesh. If anyone else thinks he may have confidence in the flesh, I more so: circumcised the eighth day, of the stock of Israel, of the tribe of Benjamin, a Hebrew of the Hebrews; concerning the law, a Pharisee; concerning zeal, persecuting the church; concerning the righteousness which is in the law, blameless" (Phil. 3:4–6).

Being zealous for the Law, Paul was known for making "havoc of the church, entering every house, and dragging off men and women, committing them to prison" (Acts 8:3). Now he was on his way to Damascus to hunt believers who were fleeing Jerusalem because of the persecution he was imposing. Only a few days prior he stood by with hearty approval as Stephen, the church's first martyr, was stoned to death. Now his zeal for God's laws drove him to pursue, imprison, and hopefully execute all who named the name of Christ.

In one instant the reckoning came. The "truths" that had Paul convinced to condemn believers collapsed like a house of cards. Thrown from his horse, he was blinded with a heavenly flood of glorious light. Imagine the stunned Pharisee hearing the voice of the Alpha and Omega calling him to account. His encounter with the risen Christ exposed him. This Jesus, the One he was persecuting, revealed Himself as the God Paul thought He was serving—a God he actually didn't know at all. He was working hard for God, but he didn't *know* God.

It took three days for Paul to process this new revelation. As his physical sight was restored, his spiritual eyes were also opened. Scales fell from his eyes and his heart as he bowed his knee to Jesus as Lord.

Eventually Paul's shock morphed into a desperate desire to know God more. "Who are You, Lord?" were the first words he ever spoke to Jesus (Acts 9:5). These words would define his chief pursuit for the rest of his life: to know God ever more deeply and intimately. In his letter to the Philippians, more than twenty-five years after his conversion, Paul wrote, "I also count all things loss for the excellence of the knowledge of Christ Jesus my Lord, for whom I have suffered the loss of all things, and count them as rubbish, that I may gain Christ" (Phil. 3:8). Paul had exchanged his impeccable résumé for a relationship with the divine! He continues, "*That I may know Him* and the power of His resurrection, and the fellowship of His sufferings, being conformed to His death....Brethren, *I do not count myself to have apprehended*" (Phil 3:10, 13, emphasis added). Paul, the mature apostle and author of almost two-thirds of the New Testament, upon nearing the end of his life, makes this stunning confession: *I have not yet fully apprehended the knowledge of God.* If this was Paul's heart posture, how much more should it be ours?

I propose that Paul set the pattern of pursuit for all believers. We are to seek the knowledge of God all the days of our lives. We don't come to know God when we meet Him at salvation; rather, we are to pursue the knowledge of Him all the days of our lives. And after a life of continual pursuit, we're only just beginning (Ps. 145:3).

My hope is that in the same way Paul embarked on a journey into light, you too will launch your own journey into light. Through this journey you must ask yourself, "Do I really want truth? Do I want the truth regardless of the violence it does to my current ideas?"

Let's be honest. Truth isn't always the friendliest acquaintance. Truth can be exposing, painful, and unwavering. At times it comes like a calm breeze blowing over our souls. At other times it's a startling alarm waking us from the slumber of our ignorance. Truth can be incredibly rude. Yet truth is a liberator. Jesus said that knowing the truth is what sets our hearts free (John 8:32). While deception holds people in bondage and darkness, truth and revelation release them into freedom and liberty. How we need this liberty!

Once you decide you want the truth no matter what it looks like, you are ready to ask yourself another question: "Do I really know God?" Let the question rest on your mind for a moment. Let it penetrate your heart. Most believers' knee-jerk response is, "Of course I know the Lord. I'm saved, so therefore I know Him." It's unfortunate that the phrase "knowing God" has become synonymous with being saved.

Consider how long it takes to really get to know someone—a week, a month, a year, ten years? What about someone who is infinite, uncreated, without beginning or end? I guarantee you it takes far more time to get to know God than it takes to get to know the average person. It's actually incredibly presumptuous for us to believe we know God simply because we've been introduced to Him. Salvation is our introduction to God, but it is not the same as getting to know Him at a deep level. Many believers, having been introduced to the Lord through salvation, busy themselves by doing works of ministry. They never invest time to get to know God deeply. They live on the sermons their pastor preaches, hardly ever pursuing God for themselves. I'm convinced that many who are saved and doing good works for God don't really know Him. They were introduced to God but never progressed beyond that introduction.

If this hits home with you, don't worry. You're not alone. Years ago when I first began to consider this issue of knowing God, it occurred to me that in over fifteen years as a Christian, I could not recall ever engaging in one study on the knowledge of God. I had spent much time reading books *about* the Lord, specifically what He does and what He expects believers to do, but I had never spent time studying *who He is*. Consequently most of my preaching had been about what the Lord does and what we, as Christians, should do—not about who God is.

I lacked a deep and living understanding of His nature, attributes, and emotions. This question hit me like a ton of bricks: *How could I proclaim anything about God when I lacked an intimate knowledge of Him myself?* God said through Jeremiah, "I will give you shepherds after my own heart, who will lead you with knowledge and understanding" (Jer. 3:15, NIV). This "knowledge and understanding" is the knowledge and understanding of God. I was deeply convicted as I came to grips with the fact that as a shepherd, I had spent much of my time calling people to live according to God's expectations without feeding them on the knowledge of Him.

I'm convinced the church will not ultimately do what God asks if she does not know who He is. God places the responsibility on shepherds to instruct the church in the knowledge of Him. A greater knowledge of Him will compel the church into greater intimacy with Him and, ultimately, greater service for Him.

Coming to know the Lord takes time. The knowledge of God is not something you can get on the run. It requires a reordering of our priorities to make time for Him. Have you ever set aside a few hours to just ponder God? Does it seem like an extravagance to focus intently on God for hours at a time? I can just hear the protests: "With so many of life's demands, who could possibly devote that kind of time and attention?" "What about ministry? There's a lost world that needs to know the delivering power of the Savior." "We don't need to just sit around and think about God when there are so many who don't know the Lord." "To focus on God and forget the demands of life and ministry would be irresponsible!"

Trust me, I know all the objections. I believed many of them for years. I was always hustling and bustling, doing something for the Lord. But I hardly ever set aside time to *be with* Him, to come to know God intimately.

Tell me, how can you introduce people to God if you don't really know Him yourself? Our effectiveness in ministry is multiplied through our greater knowledge of God. Could it be that our inability to keep and disciple new converts stems from the fact that we are introducing them to a God we don't really know—or worse, a god that isn't actually the true God of the Scriptures? What I mean is, if we are telling people to know God and we don't know Him ourselves, whom are we introducing them to?

A few hours of focused contemplation on God is

miniscule when compared to the size of our subject. He is eternal! Only through turning aside to see God and hear God can we truly come to know Him. Perhaps the tyranny of the urgent has stolen the simplicity of devotion God desires and we require. Press pause, unplug, and disconnect from the world so you can drink deeply of His nature. He is our portion and our reward! As the seventeenth-century Carmelite monk Brother Lawrence said in his famous little book *The Practice of the Presence of God*, "In order to know God, we must often think of Him; and when we come to love Him, we shall then also think of Him often, for our heart will be with our treasure."[1] What an incredible privilege it is to come to know the eternal God! I wonder how often we have busied ourselves with the immediate and missed out on the eternal. We can't afford to live at a distance any longer! If your heart is longing for a greater knowledge of God, you're not alone, and you didn't come to this place on your own. All over the earth God is stirring the hearts of His children to seek Him in a fresh way. But it will take time and focus. Ask God how you can reorganize your schedule to make room to know Him. Many things on which we've placed great importance are actually nonessentials that steal time and attention from the One our hearts long to know. Ask the Lord to show you. He will meet you with grace and revelation.

Are you ready for the journey into the depths of the knowledge of God? If so, let's press on to remove any barriers that inhibit our hearts from coming to know Him deeply.

CHAPTER 2

THE KNOWLEDGE OF GOD

T HROUGHOUT THE SCRIPTURES the phrase "knowledge of God" is highlighted over and over. At a glance it may seem a little ethereal or undefined. What does the knowledge of God actually mean? J. I. Packer says, "Knowing God is more than knowing about Him; it is a matter of dealing with Him as He opens up to you, and being dealt with by Him as He takes knowledge of you."[1]

The depth of this phrase is something we will investigate for all eternity. But for our purposes, when we use the phrase "knowledge of God," we are referring specifically to who God is and what He is like. Though we will explore the things God does, we are primarily concerned with who He is, because who He is contextualizes everything He does. If we don't know Him rightly, we can easily misinterpret His actions.

How often have you been confused by God's activities in your life? Have you ever blamed God when you faced life's challenges? When we do this, we unwittingly set ourselves in opposition to the very One who gives us grace to stand through every difficulty. Because we don't know Him, we don't understand His ways. And we don't understand His ways because we don't understand His nature.

Throughout the Old Testament one of God's chief complaints with the nation of Israel is that they believed they knew Him, though they didn't know Him at all (Ps. 50:21; Isa. 1:3; 55:8–9; Jer. 5:4; 8:7; Hosea 4:1). Rather than coming to God to find out who He was, they made idols based on their own imaginations. They related to Him from their own misconceptions rather than from revelation. The results were catastrophic.

A. W. Tozer, in his classic book *The Knowledge of the Holy*, says, "The essence of idolatry is the entertainment of thoughts about God that are unworthy of Him. It begins in the mind and may be present where no overt act of worship has taken place.... The idolater simply imagines things about God and acts as if they were true."[2] In other words, idolatry is believing things about God that are untrue and then relating to Him on the basis of those lies. When we do this, in effect, we make a god of our own choosing from our own imaginations. Could it be that the church has in some ways repeated the sin of the Israelites by relating to God out of her own ideas rather than out of the truth of who He is?

If we are to relate to God rightly, we must know Him rightly. And if we are to know Him rightly, we must receive revelation from the Scriptures that declare the knowledge of Him. Oftentimes we have barriers in our minds that block us from receiving revelation from the Word and going deeper in the knowledge of God. If we deal with these barriers, our hearts will be touched by revelation, and we will come to know Him more intimately.

False Assurance

Let's consider some common barriers to growing in the knowledge of God.

The first barrier is believing you already know Him.

Believers who have heard many sermons and been to many Christian events wrongly assess the depth of their knowledge of God. Their familiarity with the *things* of God serves as their basis for believing themselves to be acquainted with the *depths* of God.

However, simply being around God does not mean you know God. The church at Laodicea from the Book of Revelation is an example. Laodicea was a center of banking, manufacturing, and medicine in ancient Asia Minor. At one time the church in that city was a fervent community of hungry believers. Over the years, however, their zeal waned because they became familiar with God. When the risen Christ confronted them about this, Laodicea had a rude awakening. Jesus called them lukewarm and rebuked their dullness of heart. Though they believed and even boasted they were rich and well supplied, the hard truth was they were spiritually destitute. In their minds they had translated their familiarity *with* God to being fiery *for* God. In actuality familiarity had extinguished the fire in their hearts. They thought they knew Him, but Jesus's reproof revealed the opposite: "You say, 'I am rich, have become wealthy, and have need of nothing'—and do not know that you are wretched, miserable, poor, blind, and naked" (Rev. 3:17). These believers wrongly assumed they were spiritually mature when all the while they were spiritually dim.

Could this be the state of the Western church today? Our familiarity with Christian culture and church life can so easily mislead us into believing we are intimate with God when we are not. While God surely uses church services to draw people into intimacy with Himself, intimacy with Jesus is ultimately found in daily, personal relationship with Him, not familiarity with church, Christian culture, or knowing information about Him.

I know this was my state. I thought I understood almost everything there was to know about God. After spending twelve years in ministry, it seemed as if I had seen just about everything. I was sure I knew God because I was familiar with the Bible, understood church, and had preached many sermons. Unfortunately, as I learned in my own rude awakening, familiarity with Christian culture does not equate to knowing God.

If we can see that there's far more to knowing God than we have ever imagined, our hearts will soar on the journey into the inexhaustible knowledge of Him. But if we imagine that we already know Him, we will remain dim, disconnected from the knowledge of God.

Material Comfort

A second barrier to growing in the knowledge of God is material wealth. It's not that material wealth automatically disqualifies us from knowing God. There are many who use material wealth in moving, godly displays of mission and love. But often when people are well supplied materially, they believe they are well supplied spiritually. In the West we have equated material wealth with spiritual blessing, but not all material wealth is the result of spiritual blessing. In fact, many times those who are materially wealthy believe they have no need for God because they are self-made and self-supplied.

Laodicea had fallen into this trap too. In the first century that city was a judicial seat of the Roman Empire. Economically it was well known for its commerce and great resources. In AD 60, for example, the city was devastated by an earthquake but was easily rebuilt without any assistance from Rome using the resources it had stockpiled. The citizens' wealth gave them a false confidence and an improper sense of spiritual accomplishment. To their surprise, their material riches had no bearing upon their spiritual depth. When Jesus, the faithful witness, addressed them, He was quick to point out their spiritual lack and call them to buy the true riches of the knowledge of God.

Could it be that the church in the West has quit plumbing the depths of the knowledge of God because she has imagined that her material wealth equates to spiritual prosperity? Is it possible that the moral bankruptcy in our nation is partially due to the fact that the church lacks the true riches of the knowledge of God? I fear that our prosperity and comfort have lulled us to sleep and are giving us a false sense of security. Because we slumber in luxury, we have no sense of our great need for God. Could it be the financial shakings we're facing are God's plan to awaken a sleeping Western church from its dullness brought on by material prosperity?

Immediate Gratification

A third barrier to knowing God is a lust for immediate gratification and the compulsion to produce immediate results. Our society is built upon getting what we want, when we want it. We approach life almost as if it is a big drive-through window, ready to prepare everything we want at a moment's notice. We have grown so accustomed to getting the things we desire in an instant that we lack stamina and patience.

The journey into the knowledge of God is just that—a

journey. Knowing God is a lifelong pursuit, not something we attain in an instant. It requires time and a long-term commitment. Because so many want to see immediate results, they have no palate for the process. Unfortunately, if we are unwilling to faithfully pursue God over time, we will be unable to come to know God at a depth.

Oftentimes an individual's journey begins in a catalytic moment of encounter with God, but the fruit of that moment is borne out over years of faithful seeking. If we give in to the lust for immediate gratification, we will quickly abandon our journey into the knowledge of God. If we long for quick results, we will find ourselves frustrated because God doesn't answer our longings according to our timetable.

God loves the process. He loves truths that are worked into our souls over time. Coming to know God ultimately takes an eternity. I encourage you to lock in for the long haul and allow God to encounter you as He desires. We have eternity to thrill in the light of the knowledge of Him.

Foundations for Knowing God

Now that we have addressed a few common barriers to knowing God, let's set some basic ground rules for knowing Him. Once we agree on these few simple ideas, we can begin to construct from Scripture a clearer picture of who He is.

First, let's agree that no matter what we think we know of God, it is minimal compared to what there is to know of Him. The psalmist said, "His greatness is unsearchable" (Ps. 145:3). This means there is no end to the knowledge of God. He is immense. We will spend all eternity coming to know Him. After a billion years of encountering Him, we will have only begun to plumb the depths of the knowledge of God.

If we buy into the fact that there is far more of God to know than we have ever tasted, we will be in a position to receive far greater revelation of Him than we have ever known. But if we believe we already know all there is to know of Him, we will languish, believing ourselves to be rich while not recognizing we are spiritual paupers. Regardless of what you know, there is always more to know of God.

This first ground rule for knowing God is critical if we are going to move forward. Are you willing to accept that there is far more of God available than you know—or could ever know? If you can honestly say yes, read on, asking the Holy Spirit to enlighten your eyes to a real knowledge of God.

Second, let's agree that when we speak of knowing God, we are not talking about knowing Him in the salvation sense, but rather in an intimate knowledge sense. Saving knowledge is introductory. It is an essential beginning but not the finality of our journey into the knowledge of God. An introduction takes a moment, but intimate knowledge takes a lifetime. For instance, I have met a variety of famous people. On one occasion I had the opportunity to meet the governor of Texas. However, if I told you that I know the governor, I would be a liar. I don't know him. I have only met him. Meeting a person is not the same as knowing them.

Many believe they know God simply because they have met Him. But we cannot imagine we know Him just because we've been introduced to Him. There is an incredible journey into the knowledge of God available if we agree that we have only scratched the surface on the truth of who He is.

Third, let's agree that when Scripture reveals truths about God that seem strange to us, it is a reflection of our own lack of understanding, not of His strangeness. It's so easy to stay away from passages of Scripture that don't instantly make sense or that seem strange to us. A great example of this is the living creatures from Revelation 4. Each of them has six wings and is covered with eyes. To us, these creatures may seem very strange. To God, they are normal.

This begs the question, "What is normal?" I propose that God is the standard, not us. Whatever is strange to us about God is a reflection of our own lack of understanding. There are an infinite number of details about God, yet He has chosen to reveal only a select few details about Himself to us in the Scriptures. Whatever He has revealed must be of utmost importance or else He would not have put it there. Therefore, when we come across something that seems strange to our natural minds, it is an opportunity for us to journey beyond what is familiar to see Him as He is. This is how we come to know God more: by leaving the familiar in favor of greater knowledge of Him.

Lastly, let's agree that all spiritual warfare is designed to attack the knowledge of God. The apostle Paul said a key component of His ministry was "casting down arguments and every high thing that exalts itself *against the knowledge of God*" (2 Cor. 10:5, emphasis added). Wherever the knowledge of God is under attack, the enemy is at work.

Does it surprise you to learn that the devil is not firstly trying to destroy you—that instead he's trying to destroy the knowledge of God? It's true, and here's why. Where the truth of God is veiled, there is bondage, but where the truth of God is known, there is liberty. If people don't know God, they cannot experience His saving power, partake of His nature, or experience His love. As a result, "people are destroyed from lack of knowledge" (Hosea 4:6, NIV).

So while the enemy *is* trying to destroy people, his chief mode of operation is getting us to believe lies about God. In marring the knowledge of God, he can blind and bind people and ultimately destroy them. The knowledge of God is therefore the key issue as it relates to spiritual warfare.

There is a vast ocean of understanding available for you in the knowledge of God. Understanding Him is the key to causing our hearts to soar, thwarting the works of the enemy, and ultimately causing our lives to make sense. Read on, and let's take a step deeper into what the Bible says about God.

CHAPTER 3

HIS GREATNESS IS
UNSEARCHABLE

WHEN WE TOUCH the biblical truths of who
God is, our hearts will swell. How great is our
God! How immense are His ways! Our frame
is designed to respond to every new revelation of Him.
We are made to thrill at each new glimpse. When we
encounter the magnificent One in any one of His attributes, we are made to soar with delight. A. W. Pink was
right in saying, "Happy the soul that has been awed by
a view of God's majesty, that has had a vision of God's
awful greatness."[1]

Unfortunately many believers don't feel happy or like
they're soaring spiritually. Instead they feel dull and disconnected. One of the reasons we experience spiritual
dullness is because we have a diminished view of God.
When we are darkened in our understanding of Him, our
hearts become dim and we become bored. Eternity has
been deposited within our hearts (Eccles. 3:11). We all have
an inner recognition that we were made for more than the
natural realm. When we live disconnected from this truth,
we become stifled, spiritually stagnant. Perhaps it's just as
A. W. Tozer said: "The Church has surrendered her once
lofty concept of God and has substituted for it one so low,
so ignoble, as to be utterly unworthy of thinking, wor-
shiping men.... With our loss of the sense of majesty has

come the further loss of religious awe and consciousness of the divine Presence."[2] We must regain a sense of awe and fascination toward God so that we run headlong into the vast expanse of Him, once again trembling in wonder at His majesty.

My journey into the knowledge of God ignited when I began to study His attributes. An attribute of God is simply something God has revealed about Himself. These aren't personality traits but rather facets of His nature. Each of His attributes is infinite in its scale and intensity because God is infinite. He is the origin and definition of each. In fact, He is the definer of *all* reality. God is beautiful, but beauty does not define Him. Rather, He is the definition of beauty. God is loving, but love is not something He *does*; it's something He *is*. God is the definition of love, beauty, majesty, eternity, and every other one of His attributes. None of these authentically exist apart from or outside of God.

An important distinction of God's attributes is that He operates in all of His attributes simultaneously without any contradictions. In other words, God never has to suspend one attribute to operate in another. You and I, however, are limited in our personalities. We cannot operate in conflicting attributes at the same time. For instance, if we get angry, it's unlikely that we will operate in mercy. God, on the other hand, can operate in judgment and mercy simultaneously without any lapse. He is not moody, bouncing from one attribute to another. Rather, He is always acting like Himself, operating in all of His attributes all of the time.

Many wonderful books provide in-depth studies on the attributes of God. (See appendix.) Rather than trying to improve upon these classics, I want to explore a few attributes of God that have powerfully impacted me over the years in order to lay a foundation for the rest of our discussion. My prayer is that this cursory look at God's attributes will compel you into a much deeper study that will ultimately expand your depth in the knowledge of God.

The attributes we will consider here are God's greatness, transcendence, and love. When considered together, these three attributes have a powerful impact on human hearts.

The Greatness of God

> Who has measured the waters in the hollow of his hand, or with the breadth of his hand marked off the heavens? Who has held the dust of the earth in a basket, or weighed the mountains on the scales and the hills in a balance?
> —ISAIAH 40:12, NIV

Being a homeschool family, my wife and I have made an occasional practice of buying educational toys for our kids to help them learn while they play. Most of these toys aren't the greatest quality, but we've gotten a lot of mileage out of educational board games and homespun science experiments. One of the earliest educational toys we bought our kids was a motorized solar system. Powered by a couple of D batteries, the sun in this mock solar system was lit by a forty-watt light bulb while flimsy mechanical arms propelled the plastic planets into orbit. The entire solar system was about two feet wide and stood about a foot high—not very impressive by any standard, but it served its purpose of giving our kids a picture of our solar system and the relationship of the planets to our sun.

It wasn't until years later that I reflected on the inadequacy of that solar system and realized it was nowhere near close to the proper scale. Over and over the Scriptures declare the greatness of our God by emphasizing the fact that He made the heavens and the earth (Gen. 1:1; Ps. 33:6; Isa. 40:22; Jer. 32:17; Neh. 9:6). Isaiah declared, "Who has…measured heaven with a span?…Who stretches out the heavens like a curtain?" (Isa. 40:12, 22). Think of it—God measures the heavens with one span of His hand. But if we have a plastic solar system picture of the heavens, we will have a radically insufficient view of the greatness of our God.

When I found out the actual dimensions of our solar system and the vast expanse of the universe, my heart leapt at God's true greatness. Let's consider the actual measurements and see if the truth of God's greatness doesn't cause your heart to move too.

To do this, we need to have a little science lesson.

He measures heaven with a span

The universe is made up of all the planets, stars, and matter that exist in the entire cosmos. Within the universe there are multiple galaxies, and within a galaxy are multiple solar systems. Our solar system includes our sun, the eight planets, and the dwarf planet Pluto. The sun is the closest star to the earth and the only star in our solar system.[3] It is more than 800,000 miles wide, and its circumference is more than 2.5 million miles around.[4] Conversely, the earth is about 8,000 miles wide and about 25,000 miles around,[5] or about 1/100th the size of the sun.[6] The distance between the earth and the sun is about 93 million miles.[7]

Now, if you were traveling 1,000 miles an hour, about twice the speed of a commercial jet airliner, and you traveled 24 hours a day, it would take you 10.62 years just to go from the earth to the sun. In comparison, Pluto's distance from the sun is about 3.6 billion miles.[8] Again, if you were traveling at 1,000 miles per hour, 24 hours a day, it would take roughly 400 years to get to Pluto from the sun. Furthermore, the distance from our sun to the edge of our solar system is 8 billion miles.[9] Again, if you were traveling at that same speed, it would take you more than 900 years just to get to our solar system's edge if you started at the sun.

I know these are huge numbers. When we begin talking about billions of miles, we can't really comprehend how much that actually is. Our minds sort of go tilt beyond the thousands. But stay with me here, because when you comprehend this, you'll get a glimpse of God's true greatness.

Here's an illustration that will give you some clarity about what these massive numbers actually mean. Let's imagine we're constructing a true-to-size model of our solar system. In our model, let's have 1 inch represent 100,000 miles. We would need to get an 8-inch-diameter ball (about twice the size of a softball) to represent the sun. Now, the sun's diameter is about 100 times that of the earth. In order to represent the earth, we would need another ball, this one just under 8/100ths of an inch—about the size of single peppercorn. Since 1 inch represents 100,000 miles, that means 1 foot represents 1.2 million miles, 1 yard represents 3.6 million miles, and so on. That's right—in our new, true-to-scale model, taking one 3-foot stride would be the equivalent of traveling the vast expanse of 3.6 million miles in outer space!

Now, get this. In order to properly place our speck-of-pepper-earth in the true-to-scale spot from the sun, we would have to walk 26 yards from our mock sun, which would represent 93 million miles. To get a picture of Pluto's position, we would have to walk over 1,000 yards—about half a mile—and place a mere pinhead there. Then we would need to walk another half mile to reach the edge of our solar system.

Overall, a true-to-scale model of our solar system would cover a distance greater than a mile if every inch represented 100,000 miles. If we wanted to show the orbit of the planets along with the edge of our solar system, we would need a 4-square-mile piece of land just to illustrate it properly.

Keep in mind that at this point, we have only talked about *our* solar system. Scientists estimate there may be several billion planets in our galaxy.[10] Plus, there are millions of stars in each galaxy,[11] which gives the potential for hundreds of billions of solar systems in any one galaxy.

And it doesn't stop there. Scientists also tell us there may be as many as 100 billion galaxies in the observable universe.[12] Consider it: 100 billion galaxies, each holding a potential 100 billion solar systems. That means there are possibly 10,000,000,000,000,000,000,000 solar systems in the universe,[13] each with similar measurements as our own.

It's a lot to take in, isn't it?

And then Isaiah says God measures it all with the span of His hand—even going so far to say that when God created it, it was no more difficult than stretching out a curtain. What's more, Psalm 147:4 declares, "He counts the number of the stars; He calls them all by name." No wonder David said, "His greatness is unsearchable" (Ps. 145:3)!

Our God is vast!

Thomas Watson, a Puritan preacher, once said, "God's center is everywhere, His circumference nowhere."[14]

Truly taking Him in is, as Charles Spurgeon said, like a gnat trying to drink the ocean. His greatness is boundless! Understanding this requires us to honestly assess our own view of God. Have we even begun to comprehend Him?

A diminished view of God

How big is God? How great is He? I had to face the fact that over the years, God had become smaller and smaller in my eyes. After years of serving the Lord, it seemed as if He was only a little bigger than the devil and barely able to handle life's challenges. My familiarity with Christianity became a hindrance to a true knowledge of God. In some ways I had to start over and allow the Lord to reconstruct my image of Himself.

A. W. Tozer said, "Left to ourselves we tend immediately to reduce God to manageable terms."[15] I think many are stuck in this rut. They see God as only a little greater than a human, only a little stronger than the enemy. Of course, a person would never admit that or put that as an answer on a test about God's greatness. But let me ask you: How great do you believe God to be? A diminished view of God causes our hearts to contract and our vision to decrease. Internally we begin to question, "Can He deliver? Is He able to change my life? Is He enough?"

When we have a diminished view of God, we end up worshipping a much smaller, virtually impotent version of Him—an image that is infinitely less than who God is and infinitely unworthy of His greatness.

If you find that you have been languishing in spiritual dullness because of a low view of God, ask the Lord right now to open the eyes of your understanding and release to you the light of revelation in the knowledge of Him.

Seek for the knowledge of God, as the writer of Proverbs says, as you would seek for precious jewels, gold, or silver (Prov. 2:1–6), because if you seek Him diligently, crying out for understanding, you will begin to rightly revere the Lord and find the knowledge of God.

The Transcendence of God

> For You, Lord, are most high above all the earth;
> You are exalted far above all gods.
>
> —Psalm 97:9

In the New King James Version of the Bible, God is referred to as the Most High fifty-three times. Fifty-seven times He is referred to as the Almighty. Forty-three times He is called the Holy One. Some other titles given to God include the High and Lofty One, the First and the Last, the Everlasting God, and the Ancient of Days. Each of these titles sets God apart as superlative. He is the highest, the mightiest, the holiest, and the greatest of all. The theological term for describing God as greater than all other things is *preeminent*. God is above, before, and greater than all things; therefore, He is preeminent.

However, though it is accurate to identify God as the highest of all things that exist, that is actually an incomplete description. He is not merely the highest of all; He is also infinitely different from every other thing that exists!

When we think of the created order, we tend to think of things that exist on a continuum. We think of certain creatures as lower and certain creatures as higher. When we think of the lowest creatures, for example, we may think of a single-celled amoeba or some kind of microscopic organism. From there we would proceed up the scale to creatures that are more advanced—a worm, a bird, a dog, and so on. Continuing up the scale, we would eventually land at humans, then angels, and finally God Himself.

Of course, there would be a huge number of other creatures on the list, but for certain God would be at the top of the list, correct? The answer should actually be yes *and* no. The reason I would say yes is because God is preeminent, far above all things that exist. But I would also say no because it is completely inadequate and ultimately inappropriate to describe God as part of a continuum of all things that exist. He does not fit on such a scale because He is of a completely different order. There is the order of created things, and then there is the order of uncreated things. In the order of created things, there are multitudes of plants, animals, and insects. But in the order of uncreated things, there is only one being: God Himself.

What's more, as different as the organisms along that spectrum of the created order seem to us, the difference between them is miniscule when compared to God. When comparing an archangel with an amoeba, for example, we would think of the archangel as a highly exalted creature, far above the amoeba. If we were to compare God with that same archangel, we may be tempted to think of the distance between the two as similar to the distance between the archangel and the amoeba. However, to think of God in this way would be completely false. Why? Because He is as far above the lowliest amoeba as He is above the mightiest archangel. There is a great difference in our minds between an amoeba and an archangel, but the distance between the two is nearly indiscernible when compared to the uncreated God.

We have to understand that our limited perspective

is a result of our limited vantage point. How different a metropolitan city looks from an airplane than it looks from a city sidewalk! The same is true of our view of God. We have to transition from seeing God from our vantage point to seeing Him as He is.

It's just like when John said God was "like a jasper and a sardius stone" in appearance, in Revelation 4:3. He was comparing God to a brilliant jewel, but we must know that this comparison was immensely limited at best. The ancient jasper was a diamond-like jewel regarded as one of the most beautiful stones of the ancient world. Though its beauty is renowned, it is only renowned from our finite perspective. Jasper was the most beautiful stone John could think of at the time, but God is so far beyond a likeness to jasper the comparison is almost laughable. However, it's the best comparison John could give from his human perspective. We have to keep in mind that everything to which we've ever compared God is at best an incomplete and fragile representation.

From God's vantage point there is little separation between anything that He's created. Everything that exists is part of the created order—that is, everything except God. God is of an entirely different order because He is *uncreated*. Everything that has been made is immeasurably, infinitely below God. He does not exist on a continuum with the rest of His creation. He stands alone. He is "other than." In fact, He is more than preeminent. The word that defines His incomparable uniqueness is *transcendent*. This means God is unparalleled, without comparison, of a completely different order.

When we begin to comprehend God in this way, our perspective of Him shifts. Rather than viewing Him in finite terms with limited ability, we begin to see Him as

He is: infinite, limitless, and boundless in ability. When we see God this way, not only does our view of Him greatly expand, but also our faith in Him expands as well. The result is a cascade of revelation, like dominoes falling in succession. The truth of God's transcendence opens up an array of insights.

Here are just a handful.

All we know of God is but a shadow.

We have seen created, finite beauty, but what does uncreated, infinite beauty look like? All of our comparisons are extraordinarily limited. As Paul said, we can only see God through a dark glass now—oh, but there is a day coming when we will see Him as He is, face-to-face (1 Cor. 13:12)! The Scripture says everything in this age is merely a shadow compared to the true beauty of spiritual things (Heb. 8:5; Col. 2:17). Whatever we perceive as beautiful now is darkness compared to the real truth of the beauty of the transcendent God.

Imagine that I held before you an ideal-cut ten-carat diamond. Such a stone would be incredibly rare and expensive. As the light shown on this stone, the fire and the brilliance of the diamond would sparkle throughout the entire room. The array of color and light would be a tapestry of unmatched beauty.

Imagine now that an excited observer takes notice of this incredible stone and excitedly draws near to examine it. "Wow! Incredible! Amazing!" he begins to exclaim as he recognizes the brilliance of the stone.

The closer he comes, however, we realize he is not actually looking at the diamond; instead, he is fixated on the diamond's shadow cast on the floor. On hands and knees he continues his effusive praise as he admires the "brilliance" of the shadow.

How strange it would seem! We would, no doubt, attempt to awaken him to the true praiseworthy object just a few feet above his head, only to find him intensifying his focus on the shadow, persisting in adoration of its "worthiness."

When we focus on the finite and ignore the infinite, we are just like the man in this example, lauding a shadow while exquisite beauty is before us. How limited our perspective can be! Our best impression of God is only a shadow compared to the rare brilliance of His beauty. Furthermore, *every* impression we have of God is only a shadow of the truth of who He is. In fact, everything in this age is only a shadow compared to the ages to come. All of our best attempts to identify what He is like are in some way futile. How can you rightly define the infinite using the finite? How can you credibly explain the uncreated using examples and imagery from the created order?

The transcendent God condescends to know us.

This brings us to another incredible domino of insight: the transcendent God deeply cares about us. The psalmist says, "Who is like the LORD our God, who dwells on high, who humbles Himself to behold the things that are in the heavens and in the earth?" (Ps. 113:5–6). It is a stunning truth that God has to humble Himself to even behold the things He has created. The psalmist continues to tell us that this same God who humbles Himself to look upon His creation "raises the poor out of the dust, and lifts the needy out of the ash heap, that He may seat him with princes" (vv. 7–8). The New International Version says He "stoops down to look on the heavens and the earth" (v. 6).

Have you ever considered that the God who is supremely exalted over all stoops to interact with us? What king bows to engage with his subjects? No earthly king would ever do such a thing. But our great God lowers Himself to engage with us. The transcendent God condescends to our level in order to be intimate with us. The entire story of creation is about this exalted God who lowers Himself in order to express His love and affection for humanity.

Just consider it. It's a story that starts with God in a garden, walking and talking with Adam in the cool of the day—already stooping. Then, when mankind rejects Him, He never quits stooping. He makes a covenant with His friend Abraham and promises him an eternal inheritance—descendants in number as vast as the sand of the sea. Then He chooses Jacob, calls him a prince, and makes of him the nation He promised Abraham—Israel. Though Israel rebels, God pursues her relentlessly, stooping all the way. And then the ultimate shock: He puts on skin. God becomes a man, deity incarnate in the man Christ Jesus.

Through it all God never quits bowing to our level. When you think He can't go any farther, He gives Himself over to death. The One who is eternal life allows the throes of death to overcome Him. But death couldn't hold Him, and Christ's resurrection becomes the center-piece of the entire human story. Ultimately the story will end with God making His abode among men to dwell with us forever (Rev. 21:3)!

Why such excessive demeaning of Himself? What is the purpose? Ours is a God who feverishly burns to be in relationship with the humanity He created. He has never quit reaching down to us, regardless of how low it has brought Him. This transcendent God of infinite beauty and worth condescends to our level, humiliating Himself again and again for one single purpose: love. Everything He has done, He has done for love.

Let's take a look at His love, the next incredible attribute of God's nature.

The Love of God

Similar to most believers, I had heard and read about God's love for years. I understood it as a spiritual truth and even preached messages about God's love. I freely quoted familiar verses that declare God's love for humanity: John 3:16, John 15:13, Romans 5:8. Unfortunately, though, the love of God was a familiar topic that somehow became trite to me over the years. Whenever I heard messages about the love of God, I put them in the "I already know that" category. As I've already stated, when there is a truth in the Scriptures that we think we know, if it does not move our hearts, it's a sign we don't actually have revelation of that truth. Though I knew about the love of God, I did not have an experiential understanding of God's love. I had only glimpsed it; I'd never feasted on it. To be honest, I was so dim about the necessity of God's love that if anyone talked too often about it, I thought they were elementary, lacking any real spiritual depth. How wrong I was!

The truth of God's love for us is the single most transforming revelation available to humankind. Nothing has had a greater impact on my life than the revelation of God's love for me. It is in no way an elementary truth. It is one of the most towering truths of the knowledge of God. Understanding that the God of transcendent greatness is also the God of lavish, burning love impacts and alters the emotional makeup of those who partake of it. He is a God of tremendous emotions, the greatest of which are acutely focused upon His beloved people. God has an innumerable number of great works, yet His people are the one thing that continually captivate His thoughts. In fact, the Scriptures declare that His thoughts about us are innumerable—impossible to be recounted (Ps. 40:5)!

I remember years ago when I first began to drink of the well of God's affection for me. I had no idea of the journey I was about to take, which was actually a journey into God's emotions. I was in a difficult season in ministry. I was a youth pastor and, as can be the case when ministering to teenagers, things weren't going very well. I was in the middle of a youth ministry mutiny. Several of the young people had been very vocal about their dislike for the ministry and for me as their youth pastor. It seemed as if the more I tried to help, the worse things got. The truth is, it was only a handful of young people who were voicing their displeasure, but in those circumstances it can feel as if everyone is against you. I was wallowing in a den of self-pity, and so the problems I faced seemed far bigger than they actually were.

As things became particularly difficult, my wife and I took a date night road trip to try to ease the pain. We loaded up and made for one of our favorite restaurants, which was about an hour from our home. The place serves Chicago-style pizza—perfect for packing your stomach in an attempt to forget the problems crowding your mind. That night we talked about anything but ministry to try to rest our hearts, forget our sorrows, and enjoy each other. Devouring all the pizza we could handle, we gathered ourselves and embarked on the hour-long car ride home.

On the way home as my wife nestled quietly next to me in a pizza-induced coma, I began to revisit the challenges I was having with the ministry. My problems hadn't gone away despite our attempt to escape them. They were still looming there like a lump in my throat—except now I was also uncomfortably full and fighting off sleep. Stuffed and sad, in a moment of despair, I complained to the Lord: "Why did You even make humans? So many of us are so messed up. Why did You even bother with us?"

Looking back, I laugh at how a relatively small problem exposed my shallowness.

Not really expecting an answer, I was surprised when the tender response came: "Why *did* I make you?"

It was then that I knew I was about to get a lesson I wasn't looking for. When God asks a question, it's not because He doesn't know the answer. It's because He wants to instruct your heart.

I retorted, "God, I'm not in the mood for this right now. I've got real problems."

Once again the quiet inner voice petitioned. "Why *did* I make you?"

I answered by rote, offering things I'd heard or believed. But with each answer came a reply that flattened my notions.

My first try was, "You made us to serve You."

"I have thousands upon thousands of servant angels. What could you possibly do for Me that I can't do for Myself?"

I knew I was in trouble then. God's answer was something I had never considered.

I tried another familiar thought: "You made us to worship You."

Kindly but firmly God responded, "I didn't make an

entire race of people just so they would bow down before Me. I am Most High, even without the participation of men."

"Oh, God, I don't know..." Now I was grasping for answers. I decided to go broader, more generic. "You made us to fulfill our purpose?"

"Son, without Me you would *have* no purpose. *I* am your purpose."

That silenced me. Driving in the quiet dark that night with my thoughts, I realized I didn't know why God made man.

Then another question came. "Billy, what am I?"

The first thing that popped into my head was 1 John 4:8. "Love, God; You are love."

"That's right," came the reply. "And by its very definition, love must love. I didn't make you to do anything for Me. I made you to love you."

In that moment of disillusionment, the waterfall of revelation came: *God made men and women for the express purpose of loving them.*

Could it be?

Up to that point I had imagined God's main purpose for creating us was to get something out of us or to get us to do something for Him. But here it landed all at once: God didn't make us to *do* something but to *be* something—loved. We are the beloved of God. This God of power and might created us for the primary purpose of lavishing His love upon us and enjoying us forever.

Consider this truth as the apostle Paul relates it in the Book of Ephesians:

> But God, who is rich in mercy, because of His great love with which He loved us, even when we were dead in trespasses, made us alive together with

> Christ (by grace you have been saved), and raised us up together, and made us sit together in the heavenly places in Christ Jesus, that in the ages to come He might show the exceeding riches of His grace in His kindness toward us in Christ Jesus.
>
> —EPHESIANS 2:4–7

Paul says God has loved us with *great* love. His great love is what compelled Him to make us alive, raise us from spiritual death, and seat us in heavenly places with His Son. He did all this so that for billions of years to come, He might be incredibly kind and merciful to us.

God created you and saved you to express the most central facet of His nature toward you: *love.* Forever His chief desire is to lavish you with loving-kindness, grace, and tender mercy. He didn't make you to perform for Him. He didn't make you to work for Him. He didn't even make you to worship Him. He made you to be loved by Him, and it's from this position of experiencing the transformational power of God's love that we are meant to respond to Him with love, service, and worship.

John said it this way: "We love Him because He first loved us" (1 John 4:19). And again: "How great a love the Father has bestowed on us, that we would be called the children of God" (1 John 3:1, NAS).

This is why Paul prayed for the church to know the "width and length and depth and height" of the love of God (Eph. 3:18). Without a living revelation of God's love, we will try to find fulfillment in counterfeit affections and interests. So many Christians are sidetracked with sports, entertainment, business, and busyness, trying to scratch the itch in their souls that's telling them they were made for more than this world has to offer. They run around trying to fill the void, not realizing the very thing that will cause their hearts to soar is available to them in the love of God. If they will only slow down and allow the Lord to speak His tender words of desire to them, they would come to realize that the very reason they exist is because a God of burning desire fervently wants to engage their hearts! It is our portion forever to experientially know the love that God has for us. It's a love that is infinite, perfect, and overwhelming—and it's for you.

The entire story of Scripture is a love story. It is the story of God's unending, unfailing love for man. Though man has continued to resist His every advance, God still patiently and persistently pursues.

Do you know God's love for you? Have you experientially encountered the love of God? Since that night in the car I have realized it is essential for me to continually meditate on the Scriptures that declare God's love for me in order to grow in revelation of it. When I do not sense God's affection or when I lack a revelation of His emotions, it's usually because I've not spent time lately meditating on the Scriptures that declare them. If you have never experientially come to know the overwhelming love of God for you, it is yours for the taking. I encourage you to begin to study the Scriptures that declare His love and emotions toward you. Look in a concordance for words such as *will, desire,* and *delight.* These words explain what God wants and what He enjoys. For instance, Psalm 16:3 says, "As for the saints who are on the earth, 'They are the excellent ones, in whom is all my delight.'" There are scores of verses just like this one that express God's emotions and delight in us. As you meditate on these verses, I have no doubt that you will find your heart moved under the influence of God's heavenly affections. This is your portion: to know His love intimately, deeply, eternally.

The apostle John explained that when we come to know the love of God, we become fearless even in judgment (1 John 4:16–18). What could be more intimidating than standing before the judgment seat? However, when we come to know the love of God, we will stand with confidence before the fiery eyes of our transcendent God at the judgment seat. Perfect love casts out all fear.

Putting It All Together

After considering these three attributes of God, I hope your mind is stirring and your heart is moving in recognition of God's immensity. The transcendent God of colossal greatness is absolutely enthralled and deeply desirous of you. He loves you with an everlasting love, and He is drawing you to Himself with loving acts of kindness so that He can continue to show you His kindness and grace forever.

God is not eluding you, nor is He hiding from you. On the contrary, He wants to be found by you. He wants to be known by you. He is available to any who seek Him. His promise to Israel years ago remains available for us today: "You will find Him if you will seek Him with all your heart and with all your soul" (Deut. 4:29).

It is a huge step to come to know God as He is rather than who we think Him to be. But it is absolutely essential for us to see God as He is if we are to come to know Him intimately. Furthermore, our perceptions about everything change when we perceive God rightly. It is through a correct knowledge of Him that we can rightly assess the world around us. In fact, our view of everything is dependent upon our view of God, as we will soon see.

Knowing God according to His attributes is a lifelong, even eternity-long, journey that all the redeemed get to travel. I pray that you will make it your aim to study the attributes of God and that your heart will soar as you encounter greater and greater revelations of our great God. Our purposes in this book, however, take us along a slightly different path than pursuing each of God's attributes. We are going to investigate God through often-overlooked means. He has left us incredible illustrations of Himself in unexpected places by which we can come to know Him more deeply and live more fully the way He always intended for us. Let's begin that exploration now.

CHAPTER 4

LIFE'S JOURNEY INTO THE KNOWLEDGE OF GOD

N OW THAT WE have discussed the greatness of our God and the fact that He is a God of infinite love, let's turn our attention to the various institutions of life. The Scriptures aren't the only place where God declares the knowledge of Himself. He has painted a portrait of Himself throughout creation as well. Always desiring to be known by man, God has not left us without a witness. For centuries philosophers and theologians alike have emphasized how God testifies of Himself through nature. The Scriptures bear this out many times: "The heavens declare the glory of God; the skies proclaim the works of his hands" (Ps. 19:1, NIV).

Even nature, while an incredible testimony of God's greatness, is not the sole created source of His image. God's imprint is also found in every nook and cranny of life. Richard Foster said, "The discovery of God lies in the daily and the ordinary.... If we cannot find God in the routines of home and shop, then we will not find Him at all."[1]

Every one of our relationships has God's impression upon it. In fact, as we will soon see, God designed *every* relational institution in our lives to teach us about Himself. Unfortunately we have overlooked the obvious and instead approached most areas of life in ways that highlight our own roles or responsibilities above anything else. In doing so, we improperly focus on ourselves—we emphasize growing as individuals or bettering ourselves—and miss much of God's intention for the institutions He's created.

For instance, in marriage and family we tend to focus on how we can have a better marriage or be a better parent, and we miss God's primary intention for us in these relationships. Because we are unclear on this, the desired end becomes having a happy marriage or raising good children. We then work toward these ends by "bettering ourselves" so we can be "successful." Our approach to these relationships becomes one of an athlete training to win a race or a student studying to pass a test—we feel that if we practice properly or study the right lessons, we will succeed.

I would suggest that our focus in most areas of life has been misplaced and that our goals have been overly self-centered. I am in no way suggesting we should abdicate our responsibilities in any area. I am, however, suggesting that the path to growth and blessing in every area is not found by focusing on personally bettering ourselves. Peter said, "His divine power has given to us all thing that pertain to life and godliness, *through the knowledge of Him*" (2 Pet. 1:3, emphasis added). Focusing on ourselves to attain success in any area of life overlooks this essential truth: everything in life is designed to declare the knowledge of God. This paradigm gives us the proper foundation for growth and blessing; only through the knowledge of God will we find success in any area of life.

What if God's chief purpose in all of life's institutions is different than we've imagined? What if God isn't interested in our becoming good parents, spouses, or employees—at least not primarily? I'm not saying He wants us to be bad parents or spouses, but what if His primary purpose is a much deeper, richer goal?

I propose that God created all of life's relationships and institutions with one chief end in mind: to declare Himself to us. In our jobs, our families, our friendships, and our ministries, God means to—and always is—speaking of Himself. Then, when we see Him as Father, Son, husband, minister, and steward, our role in each and our approach to each dramatically changes. For instance, when we see the role of the father in the family as a picture of the heavenly Father, the way we go about fathering takes on new meaning. When we see the role of the husband in the marriage as a picture of Jesus, our heavenly Bridegroom, our approach to marriage changes. Through the revelation of God all of life's relationships and institutions begin to make sense. Ultimately these areas of our lives are transformed.

Focusing on yourself doesn't revolutionize any area of your life. Transformation only happens through the knowledge of God. That's right—the key to transformation is not trying to improve yourself, but rather to know God. While I agree there is always room for personal development and that as people apply themselves in any area, they will experience growth, it is only by God's grace that we are enabled beyond our human capacities. Through humbly seeking to know God more His grace is multiplied in our lives (2 Pet. 1:2). It's not about bettering ourselves; rather, it's about coming to know Him more.

Let me illustrate. When my children were younger, I lacked the patience to calmly deal with them. Toddlers have a way of mustering up unforeseen frustrations, and as a young father I was ill equipped to handle the challenges. I acted in ways that were coarse and insensitive to my wife and children. Though I had listened to many teachings on parenting, I lacked the critical component of patience that is so essential in child rearing.

One day as I was studying 1 Corinthians 13—the love chapter—patience, the first facet of love, stuck out to me. I began to picture all the times the Lord had been patient with me. I began to see Him as the patient Father, bearing with me through every one of my weaknesses, fears, and sins. As I remembered how He patiently ministered to me in my immaturity, my heart broke. Not only was I moved at the recognition of God's tender patience in His dealings with me, but I was also filled with vision to be a more patient father toward my children. What's more, grace for patience began to fill my soul through the knowledge of God. That day began a transformation in me that has enabled me to be patient through trying moments with my children in ways I never could have before. I still have plenty of room to grow, but the glimpse of God's patience that day changed me. It was through focusing on God—not myself—that I was transformed.

God is not looking to make a better you. He's looking to transform you by conforming you to the image of His Son. Transformation, then, is not found through focusing on yourself; it's found through knowing Jesus. Paul said it this way: "But we all, with unveiled face, beholding as in a mirror the glory of the Lord, are being transformed into the same image from glory to glory, just as by the Spirit of the Lord" (2 Cor. 3:18). The more we behold Jesus, the more we become like Him.

To sum up, your betterment will not primarily come through hard work or training. It will come through a journey into an experiential knowledge of God. This journey will see you conformed to the image of God's

Son because as we grow in the knowledge of God, we become partakers of the divine nature (2 Pet. 1:4). What an incredible promise! As we gaze on our glorious God we are actually transformed into His image.

Redefining Success

Our culture tells us that success in life is based upon performance, position, and possessions. There are huge flaws in this mentality that lead to deep emotional brokenness. Many base their self-worth upon their performance—they think if they perform well, they are successful, and if they perform poorly, they are a failure. Most who base their worth upon their performance struggle with shame and pride—shame because of supposed failures and pride because of supposed successes.

What if success in life has nothing to do with your performance but rather the depth of your knowledge of God?

Unfortunately this worldly paradigm has hit church culture too. Those with larger ministries are considered successful, and those with smaller ministries are considered less successful.

I want to point you to Moses's leadership structure as a means of dismantling this nonsensical paradigm. God instructed Moses to appoint leaders over tens, fifties, hundreds, and thousands. This means that certain leaders were specifically called to lead a group of ten while others were called to lead a group of a hundred and still others, groups of a thousand. Was the leader of a group of ten less successful than the leader of a thousand? Or are numbers a completely wrong standard by which to measure success? If the leader of ten is supposed to lead ten and is completely faithful in leading his ten, is he somehow unsuccessful because he only leads ten? What a farce! His position as a leader of ten or ten thousand makes him no less or more successful to God. What *does* make him successful is his faithfulness and intimacy with God. Faithfulness is what determines a man's position in the kingdom, not the extent of his ministry sphere. A man is no more successful than who he is in God's eyes.

When we are faithful to God in work, in marriage, and in parenting, then we experience true success. And our faithfulness in these areas is directly linked to whether or not we know Him in these areas. Whether or not we are "good" at them is secondary.

Ultimately we must come to grips with this: success in life is not found in the amount of money you have, your status in society, your expertise as a parent or spouse, or any other human accomplishment. The goal of life is not to be naturally successful but to come to know God. Success in life, then, is ultimately determined by the depth of your knowledge of God, for the more you know Him, the more you will become like Him.

Abundant Life

Success in life for the believer is what Jesus called an "abundant life." Many have misunderstood abundant life to be about possessions. However, Jesus never measured anyone's success by the number or quality of their possessions. Christ was clear: "One's life does not consist in"—is not measured by—"the things he possesses" (Luke 12:15).

How, then, is the abundant life that Jesus promised measured? The abundant life is a life full of the knowledge of God. It's not about how many things you possess but how much of God you possess. Jesus came to give us life—*His* life. Abundant life, then, is primarily about Him giving us Himself.

> In Him was life, and the life was the light of men.
> —JOHN 1:4

> He who has the Son has life; he who does not have the Son of God does not have life.
> —1 JOHN 5:12

It amazes me how many Christians consider possessions and temporal wealth to be a litmus test for spirituality. This is a horrific error. Jesus Himself, the greatest gift heaven could offer, has been freely poured out for us that we might be partakers of Him and experience life abundantly. Abundant life is found in knowing Jesus.

We don't have to wait for eternity to experience this abundant life. When we experience the life of Jesus flowing through our families and our jobs, we experience abundant life. Abundant life is experiencing the life of God—eternal life—in this age. Jesus explained that there is one way to experience this abundant, eternal life: "This is eternal life, that they may *know You* the only true God, and Jesus Christ whom you have sent" (John 17:3, emphasis added). It's as simple as that. Abundant life is found through the knowledge of God!

So we see that God's purpose for all of life's relationships and institutions is chiefly to give testimony of Himself. Through them all He is inviting us to know Him more. We live in a virtual playground of pictures that continuously declare the nature of our great God. I invite you to seek Him out through finding Him in life's institutions, that you may know Him more richly and deeply.

In fact, from this point forward, we will investigate

how God has woven together the fabric of life to declare the knowledge of Himself. We will take a look at who God is through the key institutions of marriage, parenting, ministry, and money. As we settle the issue that God has constructed all the institutions of life to invite us into the knowledge of Himself, we will find that our participation in each of these institutions takes on a completely different meaning. Whether or not things "go well" is secondary to His primary purpose, which is inviting us into deep relationship. J. I. Packer offered this explanation: "Once you become aware that the main business that you are here for is to know God, most of life's problems fall into place of their own accord."[2] Marriage is the first institution we will examine and perhaps the one that offers us the most vivid depiction of God. Let's consider who He is as we put the institution of marriage under the microscope.

PART II

GOD AND MARRIAGE

CHAPTER 5

WHO IS GOD IN MARRIAGE?

M ARRIAGE IS A mystery. Paul declared it, and those who have tasted it know this to be true. Marriage is a relationship that we choose, yet once we enter into it, it can seem to have actually chosen us. The mystery is grand, like a majestic mountain towering above the horizon with adventures untold. It beckons would-be climbers to scale its magnificent heights and encounter its beauty and glory.

Marriage is a journey, a voyage, and at times a collision—a beautiful collision, but a collision nonetheless. As author Mike Mason says, "Marriage is not a joining of two worlds, but an abandoning of two worlds in order that one new one might be formed."[1] In marriage we pledge our love and faith to another with the outcome being the knitting of our souls. Paul's description of marriage as a mystery was an incredible understatement! Marriage takes us to the heights of suspense, the depths of discovery, and the greatest lengths of wonder—a mystery indeed.

What's more, the central facet of the mystery isn't even the human component. Rather it is the fact that every marriage is a living emblem of Jesus our Bridegroom and His fervent desire for His bride. This enigma is one that will take an eternity to rightly comprehend. It's a riddle with the most towering implications. What does it look like for humanity to be joined with Divinity forever?

In our investigation of marriage we need to turn our attention to the first human marriage to discover the truths that instruct us of God's nature and His original design for this powerful institution. Before we turn there, I want to remind you of a key point from earlier. Remember how we mentioned that our familiarity with a subject can sometimes cloud the truth of it? The story of the garden can be like that. We may believe we have the full picture of Adam and Eve in that original paradise, but I propose there is far more revelation of the nature of God found in the design of our first parents and their surroundings than we have imagined. Let's approach this story anew asking the Lord to release fresh revelation.

The God Who Plants Gardens

Have you ever wondered what the garden was like before sin left its curse upon creation? What was the atmosphere of the earth like before rebellion separated us from intimacy with our Creator? What were the trees, grass, flowers, and fruit like? What about the air, water, and soil? They were not like what we have today. All the elements and vegetation of creation were wonderfully *alive*. The very air was alive. In fact, all of creation was animated, coursing with the presence of God.

Of course, we understand that every living thing is naturally alive. But everything we have ever seen is merely a shell of its former glory. All we have ever experienced in creation is under that original curse. What was it like before the curse, before sin? God's glory drenched the ground. The entire atmosphere was simmering with the life of God. I imagine the grass moved and the trees swayed with heavenly vitality.

Have you ever taken off your shoes and walked barefoot through the afternoon grass? Zoysia grass is an incredibly soft, lush grass native to the southeast United States. I remember as a teen experiencing zoysia for the first time. It felt like I was walking on cotton. I was used to scratchy, irritating fescue. Oh, but zoysia was incredible—soft and tender, like a carpet of felt. Wonderful!

But here's the truth. No matter how amazing zoysia grass is, the nicest patch of zoysia that I've experienced is actually the cursed version, far inferior to its original form. Can you imagine what the grass was like in the garden? Silky smooth and alive with the glory of God! Maybe it even moved with life beneath the first couple's feet like a foot massage wherever they stepped. Perhaps the concept of trees "clapping their hands" (Isa. 55:12) isn't so far-fetched when you think about the life of the garden.

What was fruit like before there was a curse? Think about the sweetest summer grapes you've ever eaten, ripened to perfection. As you pop them in your mouth, the candied juices rupture with a burst of refreshment. Again, recognize this: the best grapes you've ever eaten are the cursed version, only a shadow of what Adam and Eve enjoyed in the garden.

What were their grapes like? I imagine all the fruits were far bigger, sweeter, and more fragrant than anything we've ever known. Perhaps they were softball-sized, bountiful and full of nectar that would put to shame the best produce of our vines today. How large were the clusters? I imagine Adam hoisting a single cluster over his shoulder just to carry it—no holding these "glory" grapes in the palm of your hand!

What were the sounds of birds' songs like? I love the springtime songs of birds awakening from winter's rest. The life of their melodies fills the air, rousing the long-dormant earth. But what was it like in the garden? Undoubtedly the birdsongs we hear today are like the croaks of a frog compared to the orchestra of melody that took place in that day.

This conversation reminds me of our tenth wedding anniversary. My wife and I wanted to make a memory, so we splurged and took a trip to Maui. We had never been to Hawaii, and Maui did not disappoint. We had an incredible time taking in the beauty of that paradise.

On our first night there, while we were on our way to dinner, the sun was beginning to set on the western horizon. We had both seen sunsets many times, but what we saw next blew our minds. As the sun began to dip into the ocean, an array of colors exploded across the sky. Red, orange, purple, gold—many and varied hues—instantly painted the sky. Like a brilliant canvas at the command of a skillful artist, it was a masterpiece of light and color.

It was easy to tell who the tourists were that day. I pulled the car over and began to take pictures. I had never seen anything like it. It was the most beautiful sunset I'd ever witnessed. I came to find out that sunsets like this are normal for the island. Every night that week a comparable scene took place as the sun nestled low in the western sky. For us it was a once-in-a-lifetime excursion we will never forget. The beauty of the scenery and the glory of each sunset are indelibly emblazoned upon our minds.

But this truth remains: the profound beauty of every

sunset we saw that week, as well as every sunset we have and will ever experience in this age, is dwarfed by the beauty of the sunsets Adam and Eve drank in. I imagine they were accustomed to a light show of grandeur every night, the sky sparkling with brilliant tones of color, fully alive with God's presence and majesty.

No matter how grandly I describe it, I'm sure I'm not doing justice to the beauty of the Garden of Eden. The magnificence and splendor that were the Garden of Eden were superior in every possible way to the state of the earth now. The exquisite beauty, sound, sights, and fragrance were a masterpiece of creation fashioned by God to bring pleasure to our first parents.

What's more, in fashioning the garden, God was instructing our hearts in something far greater: His own makeup. Consider the disposition of the God who began creation in this way. He fashioned a man and a woman and put them in a place of resplendent beauty. What was He saying about Himself in doing so? That He is a God of passionate creativity, pleasure, and romance, a God of beauty and delight. That He desires His people to know Him this way and to enjoy Him and His creation deeply.

Imagine the intimacy Adam and Eve shared in this environment of perfection. The Scripture says they lived in this paradise uninhibited, naked and not ashamed (Gen. 2:25). The reason they were unclothed was because they didn't see the need for covering; they had no sense of shame.

This tells us much about the status of their hearts. They were free and alive!

The intimacy Adam and Eve shared portrays God's great intention for humanity. Just as that first couple was without shame in a place of pure delight, God desires us to experience beauty and delight at the highest measure too as we intimately and unashamedly relate to Him.

How different this picture is from our day-to-day experience now. How corrupting is the power of sin! Oh, for the day when the veil is taken away and our eyes behold God for the very first time! What will it be like to peer upon the One who is beauty? In fiery brilliance God's glory will shine forth and fill our entire being. This is our portion and our destiny: to drink in His beauty and engage with Him in unrestricted intimacy.

We Are Image Bearers

When God created the animals, birds, and fish, He spoke directly to the sea and the ground, and each brought forth what He commanded. In contrast, when God created humanity, He spoke to Himself: "Let us make man in our image, in our likeness, and let them rule" (Gen. 1:26, NIV). This difference may seem subtle, but it is of supreme importance and conveys a magnificent truth. Every animal was drawn forth from the earth; only humans were drawn forth from God Himself. Humanity is the only object of God's creation that was specifically fashioned from the image and likeness of God. Though our physical frame was made from dust, our being was fashioned in the heart of God. We are the only beings in all creation formed by His hands and not only by His words. This distinguishes man from every other object in creation. As such, we are the only beings credited with the title "image bearer."

Think about it for a moment. You and I bear the image of the uncreated God. Incredible! As image bearers, our very frames continually testify about God's makeup. The implications of this truth are vast, but I want to draw your attention to one specific facet: our emotional chemistry.

The fact that we have a wide variety of emotions tells us that God also has a broad spectrum of emotions. Sometimes it's difficult for us to conceive of God as emotional because we are so accustomed to our emotions getting us in trouble. We equate being emotional with being imbalanced or unstable.

God, however, is intensely emotional and at the same time perfectly stable. In fact, His emotions never dictate to Him how He feels; rather, He is what He is—completely in control of all His emotions all the time. He is perfectly balanced and completely impassioned all the time. Everything He does, He does with fervent feelings.

It's regrettable that we have believed God to be emotionless. When we think of Him this way, we have exchanged the truth of who He is for a hollow copy. God is not emotionless; He is exceedingly emotional, infinitely passionate, astoundingly zealous—a tempest of desire, fervor, and fire. But though He is charged with passion, He never swings from one emotion to another at a whim. He is fervent but never temperamental, a perfect balance of zeal and stability.

It is from this blend that God has woven together the emotions of the human heart. The heights and depths of our emotions declare the nature of our Creator, for it's His likeness that we bear. As our hearts continually move in fluid emotions, they are forever a testimony of His own internal chemistry.

The desire to be loved

There are two distinct impulses in our makeup that identify paramount truths of God's nature: the desire to love and be loved. Not only do we desire to be loved by God, but we also desire to be loved by others. Each of us has this internal code written into us by our Creator that beckons our hearts to give and receive love. The reason this code is evident in us is because it testifies of God's own nature. We desire to be loved because *He* desires to be loved.

It may be hard to imagine that God actually desires our love. The idea that He desires or craves anything at all may seem impossible. You may think, "He's perfect. How could He want anything?" Consider Jesus's words from His high-priestly prayer: "Father, I *desire* that they also whom You gave Me may be with Me where I am" (John 17:24, emphasis added). Jesus Christ is the flawless expression of the Father's heart. This statement of His desire soundly portrays the reality of who He is: He longs for love. Amazing! The One who is love itself longs for love from us. Therefore, just as we long to be loved, He longs to be loved. The longing that He has given us for love is actually a depiction of Himself. Yes, God longs for love from His people.

Now make it personal. It's not simply the generic crowd from whom God longs for affection—it's you. God longs for love and intimacy from *you*. What could be more shocking than this? You are the object of God's desire, the focus of His emotions.

Pause and let this truth settle on your soul.

All humanity is longing for love. It's a massive tragedy that most of humanity, even many believers, spend their energy and focus trying to scratch the itch in their soul for love by pursuing so many inferior and even destructive means. By design, the human frame is aching to be whelmed by the love of God. Yet many never experience

God's love at a depth—they're always seeking but never finding the very thing for which their hearts yearn. God is love itself. And the essential nature of love is that it gives. God, who is love, is a perfect lover, a perfect giver. No one loves as He does. The experience of being loved by the One who is love itself is ultimately the only thing that will satisfy the human heart.

God longs for us to encounter and know His love experientially. Partaking of His love and affection for us, even in an introductory way, has the potential to so impact us that we will refocus all of our life's pursuits. Once you have tasted the very thing your heart was made for, every other longing becomes stale and flavorless. His love is thrilling to the soul and satiating to the longing heart. It's truly the only means of satisfaction for humanity because He designed us to ache for the very thing He alone can offer: perfect love.

The longing to give love

The fact that we are created with a longing for love also communicates to us that God longs to give us His love. He would not have made us with a longing for love if it didn't fit with His desire to love us. Because He desires to give us love, He fashioned us with a heart that craves it.

As image bearers, we are, therefore, also made to give love. It's part of our internal wiring to desire to give love. When we give love, our hearts are moved with exhilaration. There is a purity of joy we experience when we selflessly love others. When we offer love with a free heart, we experience the beauty of being designed in God's image.

Of course, there is always risk involved in loving. What if our love is rejected? What if it is despised? We often refrain from loving others because of this potential risk. I'm not particularly speaking of romantic love, either. I'm thinking of daily love that gives and serves through a variety of acts of generosity and kindness.

But the one who loves others regularly, without concern for whether it's received or reciprocated, knows the joy that comes as a result of giving. God made us to love others and Himself. We will never fully experience the beauty inlaid in our design if we don't offer love freely to others and God.

Love is the chief motivator of the human heart. Nothing moves us in the way it does. Neither riches nor accolades carry the compelling power upon the human heart that love packs. People will do things for love that they would never do for money or esteem. Sadly, in our efforts to motivate people, we often use other means, such as fear or shame. This is not primarily how God motivates. It is the goodness of God that draws us and the love of God that compels us (Rom. 2:4; 2 Cor. 5:14).

What does our internal construction tell us about God's own makeup and His motivations? That all He does is motivated by love and for the response of love. In other words, all God's means and ends are love. Love is the foundational attribute of God's nature and the supreme motivation of all His actions. Our need for love specifically expresses the makeup of our Creator: He deeply longs for love. Our longing to give love also declares of His nature—that at the core, He is a God who loves to give love. God is love, He loves to love, and He loves to be loved. We are crafted by Him to portray these precious and powerful truths of His own nature.

Adam—a Picture of Jesus

Now that we understand our frame as image bearers, let's again look at the Creation account and the first man, Adam. God created the universe and all that it holds in a single week: the planets, the stars, the earth, the plants, the animals—everything in one week. Of course, we know that God also made Adam and that from the day He breathed life into him, they shared an intimate relationship. They took walks together, talked, and laughed in sweet fellowship. It was perfect intimacy unhindered by sin or human shame.

In this perfect environment God said it was not good for Adam to be alone—that it would be better for him to have a partner who is comparable to him. Doesn't it seem odd that while Adam was dwelling in perfect, unbridled intimacy with God that God said Adam needed a partner? Was God somehow not enough? Why would a mate be necessary for Adam when he was abiding with God in perfect intimacy?

We find the answer in Genesis 2. As you read it, I want you to pay close attention to the sequence of events:

> The LORD God said, "It is not good for the man to be alone. I will make a helper suitable for him." Now the LORD God had formed out of the ground all the beasts of the field and all the birds of the air. He brought them to the man to see what he would name them; and whatever the man called each living creature, that was its name. So the man gave names to all the livestock, the birds of the air and all the beasts of the field. But for Adam no suitable helper was found.
>
> —Genesis 2:18–20, NIV

Notice that God says, "It is not good for man to be alone," and then makes clear His intention to create a helper suitable for Adam. But the very next thing He does is ask Adam to name all the birds and animals. He doesn't immediately make a helper for Adam; instead, He gives Adam this enormous task of naming every animal under all creation.

What was the purpose?

The Bible says Adam named all the livestock, birds of the air, and beasts of the field. To put this into perspective, we need to get an accurate picture of the number of animals he was working with. There are 9,567 species of birds in the world today.[2] The fossil record, however, identifies 150,000 have existed throughout history.[3] Assuming that all 150,000 were present in the earliest days of creation, Adam would've had the mammoth chore of naming all 150,000 of them. If it took Adam 3 minutes per bird to name each one, it would have taken him 7,500 hours to name every bird. If he worked 12 hours a day on this, it would have taken him 625 days to complete the task. If you add in 1 day off a week, the total time is roughly 1 year and 11 months, just for Adam to name the birds.

In addition to birds, though, there are 4,629 species of mammals in the world.[4] I have read that just as with the birds, the fossil record identifies far more mammals than that—roughly 25,000 that have ever existed. If we again assume that each was present at the onset of Creation and that it took Adam 3 minutes per mammal to name each one, it would have taken him 1,250 hours to name them all. If he worked 12-hour days, it would have taken him 104 days to finish. Throw in a day off for rest and it's roughly 4 months to name just the mammals.

This means that if Adam worked diligently, twelve

hours a day, it would have taken him over two years to name all of the mammals and the birds. This begs the question: What was going on inside Adam's heart while he was naming each and every bird and animal? God had promised Adam a helper suitable for him. Undoubtedly this promise echoed in the back of his mind as he thoughtfully considered all the land animals and birds. I imagine he wondered if one of them was the partner God had promised. Yet it was obvious to Adam that not one of them was suitable. Not one was comparable to him. In fact, they were all extremely inferior, without the ability to communicate, reason, think, or feel as he did. Furthermore, each one of them had another of its own kind with it. They were male and female together. God had not yet created a human female, but each of the animals had its female counterpart. Undoubtedly this distinction didn't escape Adam's attention. How long did it take him to realize that he was a solitary creation, without equal partner among God's created order? And what filled his soul at this realization?

Over time I imagine Adam's heart began to grow impatient. Soon the dull discomfort grew into a throbbing ache of longing. He was experiencing something he'd never noticed before: desire. Until now he had been completely fulfilled in the Father's love and embrace. Now, with the prospect of comparable partnership, love was awakened in his heart. He was moved with a hunger for relationship. Desire was rippling through him. It was present from the moment of his first breath, yet it had never been aroused. What was once a latent, almost distant, sense of something missing had now surfaced with an obvious pang of longing. This internal code was working in Adam's heart even before he knew what the prospects for solving it were.

Once the expectation was awakened in him, longing for the expression of love ripened.

Consider Adam's journey again. God had promised him a helper, a partner, who would be comparable to him. Then the Lord had him name every animal and bird in existence, which numbered thousands upon thousands. Through years of working and searching, the longing in Adam's heart undoubtedly became volcanic.

What did it feel like to be the only human on the planet? All along Adam knew he'd been promised a partner, yet there was none in sight. He thoughtfully considered every creature, and none even came close to matching the yearning in his heart for human intimacy. Adam was completely alone, longing and aching for love. Why would God promise Him a mate and then delay providing that mate, leading Adam's heart to know longing at such a deep level?

We have already established the answer: Adam was an image bearer, a living depiction of God. More than that, the apostle Paul says that Adam was a type, or a picture, of Jesus (Rom. 5:14). When we consider Adam as a picture of Jesus, we discover this incredible truth: Adam's life and experiences were a foreshadowing of Jesus's life and experiences.

Just as David and Moses were pictures of Christ in their own ways, so was Adam. It's not that everything about them was exactly like Jesus; rather, their lives point out details that illustrate Jesus's life, emotions, and nature to us. The incredible longing that Adam experienced between hearing the promise of a coming companion and the fulfillment of that promise was intentional and prophetic. It was a testimony to all of creation of the One he was prefiguring, Jesus.

In other words, Adam's experience was ultimately a testimony of Jesus's experience and His emotions toward His people. Through Adam, God was testifying to us of the dramatic longing that is in His Son's heart for intimacy with His bride. As Adam was longing for a companion, so is Jesus longing for a companion. Just like Adam, Jesus desires to love and be loved by one who is comparable to Him. As Adam was promised a bride and had to wait until the day of fulfillment to receive her, so too Jesus has been promised a bride by His Father and waits with great longing until the day of full union, the marriage supper of the Lamb. And thus at the onset of Creation God was testifying of His love and emotions for humanity through Adam.

This revelation of God's incredible love and desire for relationship with humanity lays the essential groundwork for us to rightly understand every human relationship. It is from this place of love for humanity that God has constructed them.

CHAPTER 6

THE BRIDEGROOM'S PASSION

THE PROCESSION OF events in the earliest days of Creation emphasizes the value God places upon marriage. God created Adam as an image bearer; He then took Adam to the depths of longing in looking for his bride. He created Eve from Adam's side and then initiated the institution of marriage. The fact that God gives us marriage at the onset of Creation communicates its importance in the scheme of human events. It also gives us a hint that marriage is as much an image-bearing relationship as being human is. The two ideas are linked in Creation.

The apostle Paul, by Holy Spirit revelation, shed light on the importance of marriage. In Ephesians 5 he quotes God's explanation of marriage from Genesis 2:24 and then drops a bombshell, stating that marriage was always a testimony of God: "For this reason a man shall leave his father and mother and shall be joined to his wife, and the two shall become one flesh. This mystery is great; *but I am speaking with reference to Christ and the church*" (Eph. 5:31–32, NAS, emphasis added).

Across the earth the rite of marriage is repeated daily. A man and a woman make a vow to one another, committing themselves as long as they both shall live. She wears an elegant gown; he sports a tux. The music, flowers, candles, and ribbons communicate to every attendee this is an exceptional affair. Some ceremonies emphasize the symbol as a picture of Christ and His church; others do not. Regardless, the portrayal of Christ and His bride has always been God's purpose for each ceremony. Whether the officiant, participants, and attendees recognize it or not, this human covenant is a continuous declaration of God's plan and desire for humanity. This is the glory of marriage! And it brings us to a critical truth: marriage is not firstly about us; it's firstly about God. The purpose of marriage is not primarily about our pleasure or happiness; it is primarily a portrayal of God's desire for humanity. In marriage God is not firstly trying to introduce us to another. He is firstly trying to introduce us to Himself. Once we comprehend this truth, we will approach our marriages through an entirely different lens.

Marriage, then, is not just the natural outcome of two sweethearts deciding to "tie the knot." Marriage is a picture of the relationship between Jesus and His bride. This is a towering truth that must move out of the realm of cliché and become revelation to our hearts. No person came up with the idea of marriage; it was God's idea alone. He intentionally constructed this most foundational of all human relationships at the onset of Creation to forever testify of His desired relationship with us.

How does this truth change your idea of marriage? How does it transform your approach to being a bride or a groom? Through participating in the picture we come to know the One the picture has always been pointing to.

I know you've heard it before. But it's not simply a nice idea. It's the actual purpose for marriage—to know God as a bridegroom by participating in a lifelong dress rehearsal that speaks of our eternal relationship with Him.

This life is much more like flight training than it is like actually flying the plane. We are living in the test drive. There's a day coming when we will be married to Jesus, our Bridegroom. All of life until that day is only the pre-game. If this is true—and it is—our entire approach to marriage should shift. Rather than trying to improve our marriages so that we enjoy them more, we should pursue the questions: How can we come to know God more through our marriages? How can the knowledge of God change the way we function with and relate to our spouses? To answer these questions, we must take a closer look at who God is in marriage. To do this, we must turn our focus to the specifics of who Jesus is as a Bridegroom.

The Bridal Paradigm of the Kingdom

> For your Maker is your husband—the LORD Almighty is his name—the Holy One of Israel is your Redeemer; he is called the God of all the earth.
>
> —ISAIAH 54:5, NIV

The bridal paradigm of the kingdom of God is a viewpoint that identifies God as a husband and His people as His bride. It is not specifically a biblical term; it is a theological term that speaks of the intimacy God desires with His people.

We derive the concepts of the bridal paradigm from a multitude of examples in Scripture. As we have mentioned, we see it in Adam's relationship with Eve. It is also prefigured by Isaac and Rebekah, Ruth and Boaz, and Jacob and Rachel. Though we see it symbolically through these biblical relationships, the primary way it is defined is through God's own explanation of Himself as a Bridegroom in the Scriptures. Moses, David, Solomon, Isaiah, Jeremiah, Ezekiel, Hosea, and Jesus all used bridal language when describing God's relationship with us.

When we consider that God is the One who came up with the idea of explaining His relationship with us in bridal terminology, it changes so much of the way we view our relationship with Him. Think of it: the husband and wife relationship was *His idea* to explain to us how He relates to us. He is not primarily interested in relating to us as a master or owner. He desires us to see Him in the way He has portrayed Himself—as a Bridegroom!

Therefore, when God created the institution of marriage, the most intimate bond two people can share, He was speaking on multiple levels. Yes, He was giving us a beautiful human relationship that is the foundation of family and society. Yes, He was offering us the opportunity to experience joy and pleasure in relationship with another person. But ultimately and firstly, He was creating this most intimate union to depict His own heart and desire for His people. Marriage, then, is the clearest human picture we have of the intimacy and relationship God longs to share with us. It is primarily and uniquely an illustration of God's love and passion for His people.

Through the prophet Hosea the Lord makes a key point by contrasting the relationship of a bride to a husband with the relationship of a servant to a master: "And it shall be, in that day," says the LORD, "That you will call Me 'My Husband,' and no longer call Me 'My Master'" (Hosea 2:16). He makes this distinction because He wants His people to see Him as a husband and not a master. He is not looking at us as servants or slaves.

It's not that we don't serve the Lord. However, the

Lord's concept of us serving Him is way different from what many of us think. His concept of His people serving Him is that we would serve Him as a wife lovingly serves her husband. She willingly loves her husband out of a desire for intimacy with him. And so our service to the Lord is principally about sharing intimacy with Him and ministering to Him in love and worship. Too often we imagine that the Lord's greatest desire for us is to make us workers who have to eternally hustle to and fro, working to satisfy His every whim—or worse, to bow down in endless homage to a mildly interested but mostly disconnected deity. Nothing could be further from the truth. Our Bridegroom God is longing for intimacy in authentic relationship with us.

He goes on to say, "I will betroth you to Me forever; Yes, I will betroth you to Me" (Hosea 2:19). The word *betroth* here comes from the Hebrew word *aras*. This word was only used when a man was marrying a virgin. It was never used if a man was marrying a woman who had been previously wed. When God says of us that He will betroth us to Himself, then He is telling us He doesn't see us through the lens of our previous sins and failures. Instead, He sees us as a chaste virgin, one who is pure and holy. This is the power of the blood of Jesus; we are cleansed from every sin and are pure in His sight. It's in this light that the Lord sees us: beautiful, pure, and wholly His. When you understand that God is looking at you through this lens, you begin to touch the delight of His heart for you.

The ancient betrothal was a time of engagement that carried a much deeper commitment than our modern engagement does. *Betrothal* literally means "true promise."[1] In ancient societies this promise was not easily broken. From the time of the betrothal the woman was considered the man's lawful wife. Right now, in Christ, this is who we are to the Lord. We are His betrothed. He sees us as pure and holy and desires us as a groom desires His soon-to-be wife.

When I first began to understand these concepts, I was compelled to seek out what else the Bible teaches about God as a Bridegroom—and it doesn't take long when you're on that journey to find the Song of Solomon. It's the most powerful, concise depiction of the bridal paradigm found in the Bible. Let's take a look.

Song of Solomon

For me, for a long time, Song of Solomon was one of those "out there" books that didn't really apply to my life. If you're like me, you may have avoided it altogether. I had read through the entire Bible a couple of times, but I had only read the Song of Solomon as part of a reading plan. I certainly never studied it. And since I never really looked at it, I had no understanding of it whatsoever.

I remember the first time I heard a message on the song; I was stunned at the depth of its message. I shouldn't have been shocked, as every bit of Scripture is "given by inspiration of God and is profitable for doctrine, for reproof, for correction, for instruction in righteousness" (2 Tim 3:16). To my surprise I realized there was far more to this book than sappy poetry. I was gripped with fervor to study it. It became one of my go-to books to read and meditate on.

I want to encourage you, if you have never taken a season to study the Song of Solomon, let this be your invitation. There is far more in the pages of this little book than you can imagine.

The first thing you have to realize is that the Song of Solomon is God's inspired Word. It is just as vital to the canon of Scripture as any of the Old Testament prophets or any of the New Testament epistles.

The next thing you have to recognize is that it's an allegory. Some modern Bible teachers approach it in a literal way; however, this approach has only become common in the last one hundred years. The primary way the ancient rabbis and church fathers interpreted it for over thirty-nine hundred years was as an allegory that represented the love relationship between God's people and the Messiah.

An allegory is a story that symbolically illustrates an already established scriptural truth. We never establish doctrine based on allegories. Instead, we utilize allegories as tools to understand truth in a more vivid way. Several times the New Testament tells us that God uses allegories to paint a picture of broader biblical truths. Some examples include Sarah and Hagar, who portray the church and Israel (Gal. 4:21–31); Adam and Christ (Rom. 5:14); and Moses's tabernacle and the true heavenly tabernacle (Heb. 9). Similarly the Song of Solomon uses rich imagery to express the relationship between Jesus, the Bridegroom, and His bride, the church. It provides us with the story line that all believers traverse in their own journey with the Lord.

The basic story of the song is as follows. We find a young maiden who is down and out, floundering in her weakness. She has worked hard in her brother's vineyards but has neglected herself in the process. She finds herself burned out and broken down. By chance she encounters the king, and to her surprise, though she is lowly, he finds her lovely. He calls her to come and be his bride. She is hesitant to engage with him because she's ashamed of her condition. Though at first she is apprehensive, the king's love ultimately wins her over. By understanding his love for her, she comes to believe in it and decides nothing in life is better than his love. The process causes her to grow into maturity and become a bride comparable to her bridegroom. The closing sequence of the book pictures her leaning upon her beloved, fully confident in his love.

This story, at some level, is the story of every believer. We are all on a journey from immaturity to confidence in love—mainly God's love for us. Song of Solomon is therefore an incredibly important book that instructs our hearts in God's deep affection for us. It is rife with powerful truths that can transform us.

For our purposes here I want to touch on just three that are emphasized in the story.

God loves us despite our weakness.

> I am dark, but lovely...
>
> —Song of Solomon 1:5

At the onset of the song the maiden recognizes her darkness. This darkness represents her spiritual weakness and immaturity. Her spiritual darkness is seen in two facets: 1) her propensity to make bad decisions because of her immaturity and 2) her tendency to wander into sin.

All born-again believers deal with overcoming darkness while resisting temptations of the flesh and mind. Though we have a willing, sincere spirit, our flesh is weak (Matt. 26:41). Because of their immaturity, young believers have a tendency to meander off the path the

Lord has set before them. But even though weakness is resident in their flesh, sincere believers have a "yes" in their hearts toward God. They tend to stumble, but they have an authentic desire to serve the Lord.

It's necessary to distinguish between a sincere yet immature believer and a person who is insincere and rebellious toward the Lord. The sincere are brokenhearted when they stumble, while the insincere justify their shortcomings. The sincere desire to serve the Lord, while the rebellious look for the least they can do to get by. A spiritually immature but sincere believer authentically desires to know God. They recognize they can't live without Him and that although they make poor decisions and at times fall into sin, they are on a journey of being transformed. They desire to be transformed more than they desire sin, and so they press past the weakness of their flesh into maturity. The rebellious, on the other hand, do not sincerely want to know God. When confronted with the challenge of spiritual growth, of being transformed into the image of Christ, they prefer their own ways to God's ways. They may use spiritual language; however, at their core, they desire sin more than they desire God.

Each of us experiences moments of spiritual darkness because none of us are completely mature in Christ. The truth that we must grasp is that although we are dark, spiritually immature, and prone to sin, we are still desirable to God. He loves us in our weakness without regard to our performance. It is not our performance that causes His affection to burn for us; He loves us because of who He is. Even in weakness and spiritual immaturity God greatly desires you and actually enjoys you—this is the beginning of the understanding of love. He sees the sincere "yes" within your heart, and though you are weak,

He loves you. In fact, He loves you the same in your immaturity and failure as He does in your maturity and victory. His love is not dependent upon your accomplishments. His love is unfailing and unwavering.

The revelation of God's love for us in our weakness is easy to hear but difficult to embrace. What I mean is, it's easy to proclaim that God loves the weak when you are not feeling weak. But do you believe He loves you when you are experiencing your weakness in action—and that His love for you in that moment is just the same as when you're performing well?

If you imagine that God's love is somehow based upon your performance, you do not know His love. His love for you is the same in your weakness and sin as it is when you are "doing everything right." The truth is, most of the time when we think we are "doing everything right," it's not true anyway. Just because we don't realize all of our shortcomings doesn't mean they aren't there. Do you think you clearly know every shortcoming that you have? Of course you don't. God sees every blemish, even when we don't see them, and He still speaks to us as the king in the song did to the maiden: "You are beautiful and I love you!"

Ours is a God who loves the weak. When you can boldly say, "God loves me; I am desirable to Him," in spite of your weaknesses and the darkness in your heart, then the understanding of God's love for you is beginning to become a reality in your life.

God believes our immature love is real.

> Behold, you are fair, my love! Behold, you are fair!
> You have dove's eyes.
> —Song of Solomon 1:15

The second key principle from the Song of Solomon is that God celebrates our immature love and that although it is small, He sees it as real. While the first principle gives us confidence in God's love for us even in our weakness, this second principle confirms the truth of our love for God even though we are immature. Throughout the song, whenever the bridegroom speaks to the maiden, he in essence says two things: "You are beautiful, and I love you." Every time he speaks to her, he prefaces his words by affirming his desire and affection for her. Even when she turns away from him in chapter 2, he still calls her beautiful and declares his love for her.

The truth is that whenever God speaks to you, He always speaks to you through this lens. He is continually affirming you by reminding you of your beauty and His love for you. Again and again He declares over us, "You are beautiful, and I love you. You are attractive to Me, and I enjoy you. You look good, and I like you."

The chemistry of our hearts changes when we understand God's dealings with us always center around the love and desire He has for us.

In the same breath that the bridegroom declares the maiden's beauty in Song of Solomon, he also declares she has dove's eyes. Doves are monogamous; they mate with one dove their entire lives. They are forever faithful to the one with whom they are intimate. Additionally doves have monocular vision, which means each eye is fixed and can't move unless the dove turns its head. By saying the maiden has dove's eyes, the king is saying she's faithful and her eyes are fixed on him. In other words, he's declaring her authentic love for him despite her weakness.

Jesus says the same of you and me. Though our love

may be immature, He sees it as real. Though an oak tree may not be fully grown, it is still an oak. Just because it's small doesn't mean it's disqualified from being an oak. So it is with our love of God. When you understand God sees you as a sincere lover and not a hopeless, insincere hypocrite, your approach to God will completely change. Instead of cowering back in shame when you fail, you will run to Him, knowing He believes your love is authentic in spite of your weakness.

God is ravished in love with His people.

> You have ravished my heart, my sister, my spouse;
> You have ravished my heart with one look of your eyes, with one link of your necklace.
> —SONG OF SOLOMON 4:9

The third principle we gain from the Song of Solomon is found in the bridegroom's pledge of love for the maiden. He boldly declares, "I am ravished for you!"

The ravished heart of God is the central theme of the entire song and the central theme of the bridal paradigm of the kingdom. God, as a Bridegroom, is passionately burning in love for us. The word *ravish* means, "to overcome with emotion (as joy or delight)."[2] God's heart is snatched away and delighted to ecstasy by you. Can you believe it? He is deeply emotional, brimming with passion, overcome with pleasure and delight for you.

The implications of being in intimate relationship with a God whose heart is ravished for you are immeasurable. How can you lose in life if God loves you that way? If you already have His affirmation, pleasure, and desire, even in your imperfections and weakness, what else is there? You have already won!

When these three truths hit my heart for the first time, I literally walked around for days with a sense of euphoria. All of my Christian life, without even realizing it, I had been working hard for God without understanding that His love for me was not influenced by my performance.

I felt renewed. I was alive. I was giddy. I had a smile on my face for days. Previously I had been a hellfire-and-brimstone kind of preacher. After I was touched with the revelation of God's love for me, everything changed. My congregation didn't quite know what to do with me, to be honest. Something had happened in my heart, and tenderness began to overtake me. Striving ceased. Now instead of serving God to get in His good graces, I was serving God because I was already in His good graces.

This revelation not only affected my ministry, but it also affected my marriage. For the first time in my life I had an experiential knowledge of God's love for me, and the lens with which I approached my wife shifted dramatically as a result. If God was saying, "You look good, and I like you," regardless of my weakness, how could I approach my wife any other way?

For years and years my wife and I went on marriage retreats and listened to marriage teachings, but it wasn't until I began to understand the bridal paradigm—and specifically the Song of Solomon—that my marriage began to grow. Understanding the Song of Solomon has been the single most impacting revelation to touch our marriage. And rightly so, for Paul tells husbands they are to love their wives *as Christ loves the church* (Eph. 5:25). How can a man love his wife as Jesus does us if he doesn't know Jesus's affection? I believe it's not enough for a man to simply know that Jesus calls Himself a Bridegroom. He must experientially know the Bridegroom's affections for himself before he can ever love his wife the way the Scriptures prescribe. In touching Jesus's deep emotions, a man becomes a living depiction of the knowledge of God in His marriage and home. Oh the glory of marriage!

CHAPTER 7

MARITAL TRANSFORMATION

M ANY MARRIAGE TEACHERS use terms such as *happy, healthy, strong, passionate,* and *fulfilling* to describe the kind of marriage we should seek. But if the purpose of marriage is simply to enjoy an infatuation or to make us happy, then we would have to get a new marriage every two to three years.

I propose the chief purpose of marriage is not about our personal happiness or fulfillment. I can hear what you're saying: "If marriage isn't about getting my needs met, then what is it about?" Marriage was never to be something primarily centered on our human wants or needs. In fact, as we have already stated, marriage is not a humanly contrived institution at all. Therefore, the human aspects of marriage are secondary to its primary purpose.

Marriage is firstly a vehicle that God uses to declare the knowledge of Himself. Secondly, it's a means by which God readies us for our eternal marriage to His Son. Thirdly, it's an invitation to experience a glimpse of bliss in intimate relationship with another—but even this too speaks of the pleasure we'll experience forever with Jesus, our Bridegroom.

Our vision for marriage must graduate from a human-centered institution to a God-centered institution. It's firstly about Him, not us. When we move from "What's in it for me?" to "What does God want for me in it?" we will find that amazing possibilities are available.

Marriage is the most foundational human relationship. It is the first relationship God created for humanity, and it touches us in the deepest way personally. When marriages fail, it's a violent rending because, as Genesis teaches, those who are married are actually one, part of each other (Gen. 2:24; Mal. 2:15). Furthermore, Paul described the joining of two people in marriage as "a great mystery" (Eph. 5:32).

It really is an incredible transaction. Consider it—in marriage, when you make vows to another human to become their spouse, you are supernaturally joined to them, becoming one with them for the rest of your lives. Now, in becoming one flesh, we understand that we don't instantly morph into one physical body with our spouses, but rather that we enter into a unique partnership with them. We become one unit, spiritually joined in body, soul, and spirit. What an incredible thought! In the moment you say, "I do," the miracle happens: you are united with your spouse.

That God would give humanity the privilege through His power and grace to be joined like this to another person is absolutely amazing! What's more, the miracle takes place simply because we say so. When two people pledge their hearts to one another in a vow, their union happens in an instant. Through the confession of their faith, they are supernaturally coupled. It's not the minister, the congregation, the wedding party, or any trappings of the ceremony that make it happen. It is the simple pledge of faith.

In the same exact way we are joined to another person

in human marriage through a pledge of faith, all who come to Christ and confess Jesus to be their Lord (Rom. 10:9–10) are mysteriously, supernaturally joined to Him, becoming one Spirit with Him (1 Cor. 6:17). Our natural marriage vows are designed to mirror the salvation experience for believers. And in both cases the pledge is what initiates the miracle.

Marriage Is a Process

Though we become one with our spouses instantly in the marriage vows, marriage is also a process through which we are progressively joined with our spouses over time. It is the same between the Lord and us. When we say yes to Jesus, we instantly become one spirit with Him. The Scriptures calls this transaction a "deposit guaranteeing our inheritance until the redemption of those who are God's possession" (Eph. 1:14, NIV). We are God's possession now, but on a future day we will be joined with Him forever. Marriage is a picture of this process. We become one when we pledge in covenant to another, and we continue in the process of becoming one for the rest of our lives.

Entering into a romantic relationship is, generally speaking, pretty easy. Each person experiences love's intoxication as they get to know someone they find emotionally intriguing and physically attractive. They feel buoyant and alive. Their interest is piqued at the prospect of the other person possibly being "the one." If the early days of infatuation culminate in vows at a wedding altar, then the journey begins. Signing up for marriage is never the challenge; showing up for it is. What I mean is, the onset is always easy, but the process is always more difficult than anyone expects.

Here's why. When two people, who are obviously different, having different upbringings, different passions, and different personality types, pledge to become one, sparks always fly. There is no easy way for two who are essentially different to become one; they are two completely different people, with completely different thoughts and habits. To complicate matters, each of you is broken and fallen. No matter how much two people have in common, they have equally as much in conflict. No matter how alike they are, each couple starts with a myriad of differences. Therefore the journey into oneness is difficult and takes time. In a certain sense marriage is a collision that takes a lifetime to sort out. Rather than each party bringing their half to join with another to neatly make a new whole, each party brings their whole and collides with the other in a way that destroys what previously existed to make a brand-new whole.

Marriage is a journey that includes departing from selfishness, putting away shame, and becoming completely vulnerable with your spouse. We are by nature selfish to the core—always hiding, preferring ourselves, and exalting our desires and passions. The journey into oneness does violence to our self-centeredness and, hopefully, produces selflessness in our souls.

As a young married man I was introduced to this painful crucible of self-revelation early and often in our marriage. Having been raised by a mother who kept our house immaculate, cooked dinner regularly, and forecasted most of my needs and wants, I was, to say it plainly, pretty spoiled. We had to do chores around the home, but they were minimal compared to what's necessary to keep a house.

It didn't take long in my marriage for my selfishness to be exposed. I remember one afternoon, as I sat in our family room watching TV, my wife was cleaning up our apartment. She began to buzz about like a bee, straightening and tidying the room around me, in and out of the family room and back and forth to the kitchen. Gradually everything she did got louder and louder. Cabinets were slamming, plates were ringing, and her normally petite footsteps were rattling the building.

Being perceptive, I asked, "Is something the matter?"

Without a look, the short, curt answer came: "No."

"Well, it seems like something is wrong, but if you say so..."

I was dull and lacked perception that my wife was frazzled by my lack of participation in our home. The conversation escalated into an argument, and I camped out on the point that she was being rude and causing disunity in our marriage.

I was fully unaware of my self-centeredness.

That afternoon typified a decade of disagreements between us. That's right—it literally took me ten years to recognize that my mental picture of participation in the home was completely out of skew because I was focused on my own comfort instead of how I might selflessly serve my wife in love. Eventually—thank goodness—I learned that marriage is not about me; it's about us. And to make it about us, I needed to make it about her.

When both partners come out of their self-serving personal preferences in marriage, choosing instead to serve the other, the journey into oneness is well under way. We must transition from being the center of our own concerns to making our spouses the center. And when this journey is complete, you'll find the entire process was designed by God to conform you to the image of His Son.

Conformity to Christ means being pressed and sifted until love is the chief governing power of your life. Ultimately marriage is designed to reduce you to love. And what does love require? All of you. Most people don't recognize that the true nature of love is to *give* everything for the one you love, not necessarily receive it. Love has accomplished what God intended when all of your thoughts, dreams, desires, and pursuits consider the benefit and well-being of your spouse first, rather than yourself.

Oftentimes people find out too late they are in love with the idea of being in love, rather than their spouses. True love gives. It is always ready to offer everything it has for the blessing and benefit of the other. Those who fall in love with the idea of being in love tend to completely misunderstand this. They imagine love to be something that will fulfill all of their wants and desires. Instead, it requires you to give up your wants and desires for the blessing of another.

I have come to realize that when most people say, "I love you," they actually mean, "I love how you make me feel. I love to look at you. I love to be around you. I love how you make me laugh." And so on. The truth is, when most people say, "I love you," they really mean, "I love me." True love, on the other hand, says, "I want to serve and bless you. I want to give to you in spite of my desires. I want to offer all that I am for you." And so when real love comes, requiring all of an individual's heart, they have a choice to make. They can either refuse its demands and retreat into selfishness or give in to its demands and find themselves reduced to love.

Many people think marriage will be the answer to their loneliness, temptations, and other needs. This is a fantasy. Rather than getting your needs met, marriage exposes your neediness in God. Wherever there are fissures in the foundation of your soul, marriage is sure to offer the necessary pressure to expose all your internal fault lines. Ultimately marriage is far less about getting your needs met than it is about fashioning the character of God in your soul.

All that God leads us through in this life is in order to cause us to grow in love and maturity. Marriage is part of this process. Jesus is looking for a comparable bride, and He uses the institution of marriage as a key proving ground to ready us for Himself. Marriage, then, is not only a picture of our relationship with Jesus. It is also a mechanism by which He transforms us to make us ready for our wedding day with Him.

Dealing With Fantasy

An incredible amount of fantasy surrounds marriage. We tend to get our picture of what marriage should look like from entertainment outlets. But most of what we see portrayed on movie screens has no basis in reality. We see marriages that emphasize romantic love or personal pleasure, while the values of faithfulness, selflessness, meekness, giving, serving, and perseverance are either neglected or completely absent. These values are required for marriages to thrive, but most people don't begin relationships with them on the forefront of their minds. Marriages don't survive on romantic love and infatuation;

they survive on character and commitment. Marriage is difficult, but the journey to finding God in the challenges of marriage and working through its difficulties transforms us almost like nothing else.

Many marriages fail because the expectations people bring to the marriage are completely out of touch with reality. They have such a fantasized view of marriage that they don't have any sense of the challenges native to it. It's interesting to note that this is also often the case in people's relationship with Jesus. At times our modern evangelistic appeals include a list of benefits prospective believers will receive by becoming a Christian. They are promised joy, peace, and fulfillment like they have never known.

However, the testimony of Scripture includes admonitions like, "Through many tribulations we must enter the kingdom of God" (Acts 14:22, NAS). When new believers come to Christ to live a happier life, they are often disillusioned when the promised blessings don't materialize in the way they expected. Instead, they experience the hardships that accompany faith in Christ, and because they were unaware of impending difficulties, they cast off their pledge of faith.

As it is with the Lord, so it is with our marriages. Many are disillusioned in marriage because it's not the "rose garden" they fantasized it to be. When the reality sets in that marriage is not all infatuation and pleasure, but instead requires each party to deal ruthlessly with their own selfishness, they become disenchanted and cast off their vows.

If you desire to be married as a means to fulfillment, I promise that you will become frustrated and ultimately unfulfilled. Marriage will not fulfill you, nor will your spouse. The only One who can fulfill you is Jesus. You were made to be fulfilled by God and God alone. Marriage is not a means to meet our needs but a magnifier of our neediness—a declaration of how much we need God. No matter how well any husband loves and enjoys his wife, on the best day he can only offer her a hint of the perfect love that Jesus has for her. If we seek to find our fulfillment in human love, we will be left wanting.

On the other hand, if you look to Jesus as your source of fulfillment, your heart will come alive and you will experience the bliss of marriage. Rather than seeing marriage as a means to our fulfillment, we must recognize it as a means to know Jesus more. In marriage we become more like Christ through laying down our lives, dying to selfishness, and being conformed to His image. It is through this crucible that you will find fulfillment in marriage because you will find God there.

It is a fact: in marriage each party must go to the cross. Just as Jesus went to the cross for His would-be bride, we too are called to lay our lives down for each other. Marriage, then, is an invitation to the cross and ultimately an invitation to find the knowledge of God through it. Thank God the cross was followed by the resurrection! Jesus's passionate love brought Him to the point of death, and through death He was raised to new life. In the same way, we are called to walk out the process of dying to self over and over in marriage. The death to self that we experience will be followed by resurrection in the knowledge of God's love and incredible strides forward in our marriage.

CHAPTER 8

THE GLORY OF MARRIAGE—
ENGAGING GOD

D AILY, THROUGH MANY ups and downs, people encounter the heart of God in marriage without ever recognizing it. Through a myriad of emotions and by diverse circumstances, God is ever at work, testifying of Himself. As we discern His fingerprints in our emotions and experiences, our awareness of Him and the testimony of His nature mushrooms. Many of the emotions we feel toward our spouses are actually revelations of the knowledge of God! Like a skilled musician weaving together notes that form beautiful songs, our own hearts, at times, "play tunes" that reveal the nature of God. We must listen attentively to perceive the unusual song of marriage long enough for us to recognize God in it.

Let's pause and consider a handful of the emotional details and experiences we encounter in love and marriage to see how they testify of the knowledge of God. As we take a look, we will see and engage God's heart.

Romance and the Ravished Heart

Do you remember the first time you met your spouse? Remember the butterflies, the dizziness, and the excitement you felt the first time he or she caught your eye? I remember as a young man attending a small-group prayer meeting experiencing the manifold sensations of new love. There were only a handful of other believers at the meeting. One by one each of us prayed the burdens on our hearts. During the prayer meeting a certain young lady, whom I had just met, caught my attention. I wanted to be spiritual and ignore her, but I could not sidestep the distraction she was causing me. It wasn't simply that she was attractive; there was something in her voice—a sweet tone that piqued my interest.

The more she prayed, the worse it got. I was simultaneously warmed and unsettled. I tried to refocus. I repented for being distracted and forced myself to reengage—to no avail. I had been determined not to let frivolous relationships deter me from pursuing the Lord, but here I was incapable of concentrating, completely unnerved at the sight and sound of this young woman.

Something was happening in my heart that I couldn't deny; love was capturing me. The sensation of wonder and desire that filled my heart was unlike anything I had ever felt. The anticipation of possibilities, the acute desire to know her more intimately, and the longing to be near her began to prevail upon my senses. For the first time in my life I was encountering the inebriation of romantic love.

Over twenty years later I am forever grateful that love barged its way into my life that day. Looking back, it seems like I never stood a chance. Love seized me, and it has never relinquished its hold.

Why is it that love so possesses and dishevels us? Why is our introduction to romantic love so disruptive? No one falls in love neatly. When love apprehends a person, it does so in a remarkably greedy way, requiring all of us. Love draws you in, captivates your senses, intoxicates your soul, takes you prisoner, and renders you nearly helpless.

Why is love's entrance so dominating? Because it isn't

a human transaction; it's a spiritual declaration. The preoccupation that romantic love presses upon us is a proclamation all its own. What's the message? *What we feel in love for our spouse is what God feels for us.* God has formulated the marvel of romantic love to express the truth of His own passion toward us. What we encounter in romantic love portrays God's ravished heart as a Bridegroom. The only reason we know the earth-shattering activity of romantic love is because God is a turbulent tremor of passion and desire. You and I feel love the way we do because it testifies of the emotions that burn in God's heart for His people. When we comprehend love this way, we come to value love the way we're intended to—as something God has authored and offered to us to testify of Himself.

Pursuit

The days following that little prayer meeting were filled with expectation. Though that young woman and I didn't know each other very well and lived in different states, the attraction was pure and necessitated follow through. The early nineties were days just prior to consumer Internet and low-cost cellular service. The only means we had to communicate were handwritten letters and fif-teen-dollar-an-hour long-distance calls. We wrote dozens of letters over the next several months and ran up phone bills that looked like car payments. We talked as often as we could, sharing our dreams and desires. The more we connected, the more we wanted to connect. It was the most natural thing to make room in my heart and time in my schedule to seek her out. Those days of pursuit were positively surreal. The more I came to know her, the more

I wanted to know. Every phone call and every letter was accorded with anticipation of a new depth of relationship. I had an unyielding desire to spend time with this woman I didn't even know just a few months prior. She was the primary interest upon my mind and the continual pursuit of my heart.

If you've ever been captured by love, you're familiar with the desire to know and the passion to pursue the object of your interest. You don't mind any inconvenience if it means you can spend even a few minutes more with the one you love. You set aside all the nonessentials to steal more time with your beloved. Obstacles are easily traversed and barriers are broken through so the two of you can be together. In fact, figuring out ways to be together is almost as exciting as actually spending time with each other. And with each meeting you think of new ways to encounter each other.

It's amazing how inspired we tend to be in the first days of romance. Where does the drive to know another with whom we are completely unfamiliar come from? What is this fervent desire for discovery that compels us to overcome every hindrance to the relationship? The reach in our hearts for another is generated from the ignition of love, but why the fascination with pursuit? Why do we zero in on our target with such a laser focus?

It's the testimony of God written on our hearts. God is a singly focused pursuer of human love. He is resolute and determined and will not be denied the love He longs for. We love to pursue because God is continually pursuing us. It's His inscription upon our soul that causes us to engage in relationships the way we do. He is after us like a hunter, pursuing us like a lover—longing for us, stalking us, tracking us until He captures us. The entire story of creation is the story of God, the extravagant lover, sparing no expense to pursue and apprehend the hearts of humanity. We are the objects of His desire, the target of His pursuit.

When we engage in the pursuit of love, we are touching something of God. It's the makeup of our Creator alive within our frame that compels us in the chase. He is the original pursuer. Every moment that we reach with every movement of our hearts in pursuit of love attests to the truth of God's eternal quest to apprehend humanity. As we pursue, we tell the story of the God who is always pursuing the hearts of men.

Faithful Devotion

Betrayal may be the most emotionally destructive offense an individual can sustain. It injures the heart like nothing else. It cuts deeply. When we invest at a deep level with someone, only to have that trust broken by disloyal actions, it disturbs us at our most basic level. Like the instability of shifting sand beneath our feet, the foundations of our heart fracture under the weight of betrayal. What we thought was solid proves unstable, and we are forced to reassess the way we trust and invest in other people. Betrayal upsets our compass, leaving us reeling, groping to find true north. It's no wonder that Jesus's crucifixion was initiated through the betrayal of one of His closest friends.

The most severe betrayal in human relationships is the betrayal of marriage vows. When an individual pledges their heart to another with a vow, the two are yoked in the most powerful way that exists. And if the vows are broken, if the covenant is severed, the hardships that ensue are unmatched in human experience. Not only are there manifold challenges in the areas of property, custody of children, and distribution of assets, there are monumental emotional and spiritual difficulties. The backlash that each party experiences leaves them deeply scarred for decades, and in some cases a lifetime.

It's significant to note that believers and unbelievers alike recognize the offense of betrayal in marriage. Even tabloid magazines express outrage at the treachery of adultery and broken marriage vows. Why is there such scandal over betrayal in marriage? Why does virtually every society on earth despise the disloyalty of marital unfaithfulness? Why is there universal outrage and disdain over broken vows? Because faithfulness is the standard we expect when we enter into a pledge, not fickleness.

So where does this internal design come from? Once again: God. Our disgust with broken vows and our longing for faithfulness in relationship is the very longing of our Creator's heart. What's more, it's the consistent ideal governing all His actions. He is faithful through and through. He is the rock, the fortress, the sure foundation. His name is "Faithful and True" (Rev 19:11). He is the faithful God in all that He says and does.

When we burn against betrayal, we reflect God's composition. Our God is faithfully devoted to His people and desires the same from us. We operate in this same mold, pledging our hearts in faithfulness and requisitioning others to do the same. Herein is the glory of marriage: we reveal the heart of God as the moon reveals the light of the sun.

Jealousy

The passions of love can affect the human heart in the most unexpected ways. Love's influence can find you floating in ecstasy or burning in indignation. Inherent in marital love is jealousy, which not only protects but also becomes possessive of love's object.

I know firsthand the possessing influence of love manifested in jealousy for my wife. One afternoon we were returning home from running a few errands when we pulled in to find several kids from our neighborhood playing in our driveway. As we drove up, through the cracked window, I heard one of the children make a very crude, off-color remark about my wife. I felt blood rush to my face and my temperature rise.

After parking the car, I jetted out to the driveway to require the little boy to apologize to my wife. He was nowhere to be found, but the remaining children told me he had run home. I bolted for his house, which was situated on the opposite side of our cul-de-sac.

A fourth of the way there a man whom I had not met before emerged from the boy's home and strode with authority in my direction. As we met in the middle of the cul-de-sac, the man told me he was the boy's guardian for the day and challenged me by asking, "What's your problem?"

Without flinching, I told him what the boy said to my wife. "I want him to apologize right now."

With a stunned look and a nod, the man replied, "I'll go get him and make him apologize."

The man made a beeline to retrieve the young boy and require him to make an apology to my wife. It wasn't until he turned to get the boy that I realized the man

I had stared down stood a half-foot taller than me and easily outweighed me by fifty pounds. He was muscle bound and had a stern look. Later, as I replayed the scene in my mind, I realized this guy could have squashed me. But instead, at my insistence, he made the boy apologize.

I mulled over the emotions I felt and the boldness I displayed in the face of a guy who clearly had me out-manned. What got into me? I didn't even notice his size as I demanded an apology for my wife. I was on fire with zeal to protect the honor of my bride. Pure jealousy coursed through me, causing me to act in passionate protection.

Where did it come from? By now you know the answer. It was the imprint of God's nature upon my soul. I erupted in jealousy, which caused me to throw caution to the wind because I'm made in the image of God, who is a volcano of pure, fiery jealousy. God's jealousy wrought in human hearts is a powerful component of love. I'm not talking about being hotheaded here; I'm talking about love that is willing to stand up for the honor of its beloved.

Moses was the first to mention God's fiery jealousy: "God is a consuming fire, a jealous God" (Deut. 4:24). He is jealous! He's not envious, but He is possessive. He won't bear sharing His beloved with others. He has bought us with the price of His Son's blood. We are no longer our own. Because God loves us, He will not suffer another to have our affections, nor will He permit us to be defrauded in any way. He is the avenger of the weak and the champion of all who suffer injustice (1 Thess. 4:6). Every wrong enacted against God's bride will be rectified. He will not allow any injustice to go unanswered. Just as a husband is enflamed at the thought of his wife being presumed upon, God's jealousy is stirred in passion whenever His people are taken advantage of. The fire of jealousy that a husband feels is God's own fire. "Jealousy is a husband's fury," says Proverbs 6:34. The fury of our jealous God is unmatched. Every husband touches the burnings of God's heart through the institution of marriage. The burning heart of jealousy that beats in the chest of every bridegroom for his bride is the design of heaven.

In this section we have briefly touched on a few facets of God's nature that are revealed to us through the institution of marriage. These depictions are by no means an exhaustive list of all the attributes of God. I'm only offering you a glimpse behind the curtain. I encourage you to consider the many and varied implications of who God is as the Bridegroom God and allow the knowledge of Him to shape your view and approach to marriage. In the next section we will press on to consider again the institution of family, this time with regard to parenting, with the goal of knowing more of God in and through this important institution.

PART III

GOD AND PARENTING

CHAPTER 9

WHO IS GOD IN PARENTING?

B ILLY, BILLY, I need to talk to you about something."
My wife's sweet voice rang in a singsong tone. I
knew this tone; it was the one she used when she
wanted to tell me something about myself I wasn't seeing.
Whatever she had to say, I knew she was going to deliver
it with grace, but I couldn't help but brace myself for the
impending correction. Whatever it was, I probably needed
to hear it. Sheepishly I replied, "Sure, Sweet. What is it?"

"I'm twenty-eight, and my clock is ticking. We've been
married for five years now. What I'm trying to say is I'm
ready to have a baby."

Instantly my trepidation turned to shock. I hadn't seen
this coming. We were enjoying what I call the "single, married life." Without kids we had the freedom to do what we
wanted, when we wanted. Our schedule was our own. We
were very involved in ministry at a thriving church. We
had lots of commitments and friends to keep up with. I
knew kids would come someday—just not *this* day.

In that instant reality landed: We weren't going to be
"single" any longer.

Within moments my shock was supplanted by fear.
The weight of real responsibility bore down on me. *Could
I be a father? Would I be able to take responsibility for
a child? What do you do with babies, anyway?* You have

to understand, I was the youngest of three boys in my family—no sisters and no younger siblings. The closest I had been to a diaper was taking out the trash at church. This was completely uncharted territory for me.

Regardless of my fear and uncertainty, it was obvious it was time. Mrs. Humphrey had made her heart known, and there would be no denying it. We would be parents.

Four children later I can happily report all my fears were completely unfounded. Of course, with children does come far more responsibility, but with that responsibility comes an incredible journey into parental love. To be honest, as I look back, I have no idea why we waited so long to have kids. Our lives have been incredibly enriched, and for us it's hard to remember what life was like without our children. I like to say we have a family love affair. Sure, parenting has presented its share of challenges, but those challenges have been far outweighed by the joy our kids have brought to our lives.

The truth is, parenting is as much for us as it is for them. In fact, there are precious truths I don't think I would have ever come to know if it weren't for God's gifts in the form of my children. The first and greatest of those truths is fathering love—something I hadn't comprehended at all until I was a father myself.

As a young believer and minister I valued fiery holiness and revival preaching. Actually I still do. I love reading the testimonies and messages of revivalists such as Charles Finney, Jonathan Edwards, John Wesley, Evan Roberts, John G. Lake, and others. This kind of preaching put a fiery passion for the Lord in my heart, but it also left me shallow when it came to other components of God's nature, like His mercy, kindness, and grace. Becoming a father instructed me in these facets of God at an accelerated pace. You could say God took me on a crash course in His tender loving-kindness once I became a parent.

A Mushy, Syrupy Mess

Shortly after our aforementioned baby conversation, we got pregnant. At the time my wife was a middle school home economics teacher. After a very rough first trimester, where she experienced daily nausea, her pregnancy was fairly ideal. She was able to continue teaching and participating in all our ministry commitments. She taught school until the day she went into labor.

I remember vividly that April morning as I was getting ready to leave for work. The phone rang. I answered to hear my wife's calm voice on the other end say, "Billy, something's happening. I'm coming home because I think I'm in labor!"

The thrill of those words sent a jolt down my spine. It was actually happening!

By that afternoon we were in the delivery room. We had worship music playing in the background and one of our closest friends with us to take pictures of our newborn. It was a very quick labor. My wife was so strong, and within just a few moments the midwife was holding our son. She turned to me and asked, "Dad, do you want to cut the cord?"

Awe filled my heart. Here he was—our son. I was dazed. The scene was like something from a dream.

I cut the cord as the midwife asked, "So, what do you think about him, Dad?"

The dam broke. A flood of emotion filled my soul. Tears burst from my eyes, and with a lump in my throat I croaked, "He's beautiful."

I didn't intend to cry, and I definitely didn't intend to call my firstborn son beautiful. Great. Amazing. Tough. Awesome. Any manlier adjective would've worked. Instead...*beautiful*. I was undone. This fiery revival preacher had been reduced to a mushy, syrupy mess. And so he was...beautiful.

Fathering Love

As I have reflected on that wonderful day and the dream scene in the delivery room, revelation has lit my mind. As I said, I didn't intend or expect to cry. In fact, to that point I would have said I wasn't a crier at all. But when those tears came, something awakened in me I had not known: fathering love.

I had known the love of a bridegroom because I was very much in love with my wife and was accustomed to the feeling of passionate love that we shared. But that day I experienced a completely different version of love. I was overcome with emotion for my son, even though he had no idea I existed yet. He didn't know my name, couldn't see my face, and couldn't understand my voice. He could barely open his eyes, and he definitely couldn't do anything for me or love me back.

Nonetheless, I was completely captured by him. It would be years until he could communicate with me, yet I was struck with effortless, uncontrollable affection for him from that very first day.

I was as surprised as anybody at the mush ball I became. Where did all this emotion come from? How could this fiery, revival preacher become so mushy? Divine design. The image-bearing imprint God had laid in my heart was operating at peak performance. As I experienced incredible tenderness and love toward my son, the Father testified of His incredible tenderness and love toward me. Could it be the reason I felt this love that seemed to come out of nowhere was because it's a picture of how the Father feels for us, His children? Unquestionably, yes!

My continual delight for my children has been a testimony of God's continual delight for me. Not a week goes by where I don't marvel with enjoyment at them—and not because of what they do for me, but simply because of who they are. If I, as a broken man with many flaws, can feel this level of love and delight for my kids, what does the eternal Father, perfect in all His affection, feel for me?

Our God, Our Father

My experience of fatherhood has brought me to this realization: God has given us the parenting relationship chiefly as a declaration of Himself. This realization set me on a journey into the Scriptures to find out who God is as Father—a journey that continues to this day.

Along the way I have come upon two keys that helped me to begin to understand God as Father. They are both found in His own explanations of Himself.

The first we find through God's interaction with Moses at the burning bush. God identified Himself to Moses as the God of Abraham, Isaac, and Jacob—the God of three generations of fathers. This title let Moses know that he was speaking to the right God. But more than that, God was forever identifying Himself with fatherhood. He wanted to be known as the God of generations of fathers. This spoke to me of God's desire to be seen as a God of family, a God of fatherhood. He could have identified Himself as the God who rained fire and brimstone on

Sodom or the God who flooded the earth in the days of Noah, but instead He chose to portray Himself as a God of fathers to emphasize an important truth of His nature: He is a father to us.

Next, when Moses asked God to reveal Himself to him at Sinai, God declared His name to Moses. He did this because His name is His nature. In that moment of heavenly glory the Lord revealed Himself as "the LORD God, merciful and gracious, longsuffering and abounding in goodness and truth, keeping mercy for thousands, forgiving iniquity and transgression and sin" (Exod. 34:6–7). These attributes are the chief components of God's nature. He is merciful, gracious, patient, and overflowing with goodness, truth, and forgiveness. He is a God of infinite kindness. But though He's infinitely kind, He is by no means a pushover. He then goes on to say He holds the guilty accountable and does not dismiss their sin. He's ever willing to forgive the repentant, and at the same time He is the judge of the obstinate.

The emphasis, though, when asked by Moses who He was, was His leading attributes: mercy, tenderness, gentleness, and compassion—all fathering traits.

This is our God. He is our father.

What happened to me that day in the delivery room was that this God of loving-kindness and tender mercy began to reveal Himself by allowing me to feel for my son the very emotions God feels for me. He was introducing me to facets of His nature I'd never known in such a personal way before.

It has taken me years to dig into the truth that God is a tenderhearted Father who is overwhelmed with enjoyment and delight for His children. Through understanding just a bit of His nature my entire paradigm shifted. Rather than perceiving God as one I have to please with my performance, I have come to see Him as the God who has loved me before I even knew His name. This understanding has settled and stabilized my heart like nothing else. It has also caused me to relate to my children in a way that attempts to portray God's heart toward them too.

When understanding God as Father, it's important to consider the verses in which God describes Himself as such. More than 250 times in the Bible God is referred to as Father—more than 120 of those times in the Book of John alone! Read a few of these references slowly, and allow them to speak to your heart:

> Love your enemies… that you may be sons of your Father in heaven.
> —MATTHEW 5:44–45

> The Father Himself loves you.
> —JOHN 16:27

> It is your Father's good pleasure to give you the kingdom.
> —LUKE 12:32

> You received the Spirit of adoption by whom we cry out, "Abba, Father."
> —ROMANS 8:15

> Behold what manner of love the Father has bestowed on us, that we should be called children of God.
> —1 JOHN 3:1

> He who overcomes shall inherit all things, and I will be his God and he shall be My son.
> —REVELATION 21:7

What does it say about God that He would depict Himself this way this often? It says that He is a Father and wants to be known and related to as such (Jer. 3:19). This brings us to an incredibly important truth: every human father is supposed to be a picture of who God is. Every day throughout the earth, the male leader of human families is supposed to be a depiction of our heavenly Father, the leader of our eternal family. The entire design of the family is engineered to declare the truth of God's nature as father.

Earthly Fathers Reflect the Heavenly Father

I have ministered to youth and young adults for the last twenty years. Over that time I have spent countless hours counseling and connecting with young people, and I can say definitively that one of the chief reasons so much brokenness exists in the young generation is because of a lack of godly parenting, and specifically godly fathering. From a young age the relationship we have with our earthly fathers speaks to us of a greater reality: the nature of our heavenly Father. Unfortunately many young people grow up believing God to be absent, disinterested, angry, or unreliable. After digging through their family histories, you find the very issues they have against God are issues they have against their earthly fathers. Much of the brokenness in their hearts stems from brokenness in their relationships with their fathers, which in turn translates into a perverted view of God and brokenness in their relationships with Him.

In helping young people relate to God, I bring them to the scriptures that declare God's nature and explain to them the image they have of God based on their human fathers or father figures is not necessarily the truth of who God is. Once they begin to see God as He is, a Father who loves them and affirms them, their hearts unlock and they begin to experience sweet intimacy with God.

The issue of the knowledge of God as Father is so important that one of Jesus's chief purposes was to be a living representation of the Father to the world. Jesus so represented the Father that He said, "He who has seen Me has seen the Father" (John 14:9). All that Jesus did and said was an exact representation of the Father's will expressed in words and deeds. Oftentimes people love Jesus as Savior but feel aloof from God as Father. When we separate the two, we fail to realize all that Jesus represents.

CHAPTER 10

THE FATHER'S DELIGHT IN THE SON

B EFORE GOD CREATED the heavens and the earth, He was. Before there was time or space, there was God. Just trying to wrap your mind around existence before time can give you a headache! But the Scriptures reference a season of existence, before anything was created, when it was just God. The Bible uses phrases such as "Before time began," "Before the world was," "Before there was ever an earth" that all describe a time when it was just God.

What was it like when it was just God—God alone, perfect, glorious, in that vast expanse of existence? Three in One, exalted, relating to Himself within the Godhead, flowing in love with Himself. It makes me wonder, what exactly was He doing? The Bible actually gives us the answer, and surprisingly it's very simple. God was doing what God does best: enjoying Himself.

God was enjoying Himself? I know that sounds a little strange, but if it's true—and it is—you have to ask, how? How was God enjoying Himself, and what are the implications of that? The answer leads us into a revelation of His heart that will completely transform your view of God.

Proverbs 8 gives us a picture of wisdom personified as a teacher. It's wisdom that describes the time of existence before Creation and the delight shared with the Father.

> I have been established from everlasting, from the
> beginning, before there was ever an earth.... Then
> I was beside Him as a master craftsman; and I
> was daily His delight, rejoicing always before Him,
> rejoicing in His inhabited world, and my delight
> was with the sons of men.
>
> —PROVERBS 8:23, 30–31

Many commentators agree that wisdom in this passage
represents Jesus, for Jesus has been made to us wisdom
from God (1 Cor. 1:30). It's as if the Son of God is speaking
in first-person here in Proverbs, describing the pre-Creation
existence He, the Father, and the Holy Spirit shared.

Notice in verse 30, He says, "I was daily His [the
Father's] delight, *rejoicing* always before Him" (emphasis
added). Daily the Father delighted in the Son. What was
that like—the eternal Father enjoying His only begotten?
Undoubtedly they shared untold intimacy and joy.

Now look at the word *rejoicing*. In Hebrew, it's the
word *sachaq*. It literally means "to laugh."[1] It's translated
laugh, play, amuse, celebrate, joke, and rejoice. The picture *sachaq* gives us is that the Father and the Son were
doing a lot more than simply regarding each other with
a pleasant look. They were celebrating each other with
joyful glee!

Could it really be? Is it possible the Father and the
Son spent their time laughing and joking in playful intimacy before the creation of the world? The answer is a
resounding yes! The Father and the Son deeply enjoy one
another. And in the "time" before time began, their chief
activity was to express within the Godhead their love and
enjoyment of each other with amusement and rejoicing.
To say it simply, they were having a lot of fun together!

What does this reveal to us about the heart of the Father toward His Son? What does it say about His heart toward *all* of His children? Is this a difficult picture for you to imagine—the eternal Father laughing, joking, and enjoying the Son? If it's hard for you to fathom, it could be that your image of God as Father has been skewed by earthly images of what a father is. The eternal Father's continuous impulse toward His Son has always been enjoyment and delight. This is who He is: the Father who enjoys His Son. And so it is also His continuous impulse toward you.

. With these thoughts in mind, let's consider Paul's words to the Ephesians:

> He chose us in Him before the foundation of the world...having predestined us to adoption as sons...*according to the good pleasure of His will.*
> —EPHESIANS 1:4–5, EMPHASIS ADDED

The Good Pleasure of His Will

When God considered making the created order, He did not look to anything or anyone else for inspiration. Instead, He looked to the one place that could offer Him inspiration: Himself. He looked inside Himself and thought, "What will make Me the happiest and bring Me the most pleasure?" In that moment a flood of billions of people was actualized in His mind and became a part of creation.

Among those billions was you. You are a result of a decision in God's heart to create what would bring Him pleasure. It was in that "time" before time began that He dreamed of you and purposed in Himself to create you and adopt you as His own child. In that season of delight and laughter He was sharing with the Son, the Father considered the "good pleasure of His will," and you came into being in the mind of God. Isn't that amazing?

When comparing the verses from Proverbs 8 with Ephesians 1, we get a clearer picture of the specific source for God's inspiration in creating you. He was enjoying Himself so much, experiencing such incredible pleasure with the Son, that He decided He wanted to have an entire family of children to enjoy! He dreamed of ones who would delight His heart, and it was from this context that you were made. What was the reason He formed your frame? To share delight. It was the laughter and joy the Father and the Son shared that compelled God to want to share laughter and joy with you. Yes, that is why He made you: to enjoy you. He is that tender and kind. If you can accept it, He is that fun.

For our hearts to operate the way they are created to operate, we must come to know and believe God's purpose for creating us is to enjoy us. So often we have believed the Father is trying to get something out of us, trying to get us to produce or perform better. He is not trying to get something out of us. Rather, He desires to experience delight with us exactly as He experiences it with His Son.

In addition, when a human father delights in his children, we see the very image of God at work in him. The reason any human father enjoys his kids is because God is a Father who deeply enjoyed His Son first.

"This Is My Beloved Son"

It is essential to understand how much the Father loves Jesus in order to understand the eternal Father's affections for you. So let's consider the Father's feelings toward Jesus. On three separate occasions the eternal Father interrupted the course of human affairs and thundered audibly from heaven to declare His love and affection for Jesus (Matt. 3:17; 17:5; John 12:28). Peter bore witness to this, and it had a powerful effect upon his perception of God (2 Pet. 1:17).

Imagine what was going on in the heart of the eternal Father that He would see fit to interrupt the normal course of human affairs and declare His affection for His Son. The words the Father spoke over the Son on two of the three occasions were, "This is My beloved Son!" That's absolutely amazing.

Now imagine a natural father at his child's ball game. The father sits watching his son play the game and is so filled with delight that he erupts into shouting. Instead of singing "Take Me Out to the Ball Game," the father shouts, "I love my son. He makes me *so happy!*" That is exactly what the eternal Father did. Not just once but on three separate occasions He thundered His delight for Jesus for all those around to hear.

It was through the prophet Isaiah that the Father first described His great emotion, and pleasure for His "Elect One":

> Behold! My Servant *whom I uphold, My Elect One in whom My soul delights! I have put My Spirit upon Him*; He will bring forth justice to the Gentiles...I, the LORD, have called You in righteousness, and *will hold Your hand*; I will keep You and give You as a covenant to the people, as a light to the Gentiles.
> —ISAIAH 42:1, 6, EMPHASIS ADDED

Consider these specific details of the Father's affections for Jesus:

1. He calls Jesus "My Servant whom I uphold." This speaks of His unending, inexhaustible commitment to His Son. The Father upholds the Son, never allowing Him to falter or fail.

2. He calls Him His "Elect One." This means the Son is the chosen of the Father. Natural parents are unable to pick their children. Only adoptive parents are afforded the privilege of choosing. But the Father has picked—chosen—all His children, including His Son, Jesus. The fact that the Father chose Jesus speaks of the Father's specific interest in Jesus. The Father had a choice in the matter, and His choice was Jesus.

3. He calls Him the One "in whom My soul delights." We have established the Father's infinite delight and pleasure for the Son. It is Jesus who moves the Father's heart and who gives the Father great pleasure.

4. He says of Him, "I...will hold Your hand." What an incredibly tender expression of the Father's heart! This speaks of the Father's leadership in the life of the Son and also the Father's caring posture toward the Son.

All of these descriptions give us insight into the Father's heart. However, the expression of the Father's heart doesn't stop with His feelings toward His only begotten.

The stunning truth is that the eternal Father loves you and me in the very same way He loves Jesus.

Consider Jesus's words from John 17:

> I do not pray for these alone, but also for those who will believe in Me through their word; I in them, and You in Me; that they may be made perfect in one, and that the world may know that You have sent Me, and *have loved them as You have loved Me.*
>
> —JOHN 17:20, 23, EMPHASIS ADDED

In this prayer at the end of His life Jesus prays not only for His disciples but also for all who would believe in Him through their witness. Of these future believers, Jesus reveals a shocker. He says, "You…have loved them as You have loved Me." From the mouth of Jesus we learn the Father loves us in the exact same way He loves Jesus. The same measure of love He feels for Jesus is the same measure of love He feels for you. The same passion and zeal He has for Jesus is the same passion and zeal He has for you. The same delight and enjoyment Jesus brings to His heart is the same delight and pleasure you bring to it. Just as the Father upholds Jesus, He upholds you. Just as Jesus is the Father's chosen child, so are you. Just as Jesus delights the Father's soul, so do you!

Come to Know God's Heart Toward You

When we come to comprehend the Father's enjoyment and affection for us, His children, then we are able to rightly enjoy and love our own children. It is only from the place of understanding who God is as Father that we are able to love and care for our children the way God intended. Without knowing God as a loving Father, not only will we live broken and fractured lives, but also our relationships with our children will suffer because we haven't comprehended the model we are to be emulating.

God gives us the gift of children and places incredible love in our hearts for them to portray to us the delight that He has for us. As a result, knowing God's heart and His enjoyment of us should be our ultimate purpose in parenting our kids. Sure, we guide them, help them mature, and instruct them in the myriad of life's nuances. But in the end God's goal for you in parenting is to come to know His enjoyment of you and for you to impart this same truth to your children by enjoying them in return.

Most of what we imagine to be really important in life is in fact not that important. Schedules and schooling, chores and training—all of these things have their place and should not be neglected, but what good is it to train your child in mathematics but leave him with no concept of the delight God has in him? Which is more valuable: a degree or a heart alive in the delight of God?

Too often we emphasize the earthly and completely miss God's design in parenting. We don't have to neglect a proper education or good discipline in exchange for them knowing we enjoy them. But we should not make any earthly pursuits the first goal of parenting. When we emphasize human achievement, education, or even morality over God's nature in our parenting, we miss out on an incredible opportunity to train our kids in the most important subject of all: God.

As we make the knowledge of God the primary pursuit in our parenting, we then set the proper foundation from which spring the other facets of parenting such as training, discipline, care, provision, and encouragement.

We should not forfeit the knowledge of God in favor of human-centered success. Let's determine to portray God's heart for our kids, while we instruct them in the rest of life's necessities. We can only do this by coming to know His heart for us first. From the well of the experiential knowledge of God's affections, we are then able to offer our children the same. It is only in the light of His love that we are able to love.

If you have children, take a moment right now and consider the delight your children are to you. For a moment don't consider their insufficiencies or any of the responsibilities you carry as a parent. Simply call to mind the things about their personalities that you love. Remember the moments they precociously said or did something that surprised you into laughter. Recall the times when you watched them without them knowing it and it melted your heart.

Now recognize that for you to love your children in this way, it is the Father's imprint on your heart and His continual attitude toward you. He looks at you with enjoyment even when you don't sense it. This is the well we are to draw from in our parenting—the knowledge of God's affections as our Father.

CHAPTER 11

THE GLORY OF PARENTING— ENGAGING GOD

W HEN YOU THINK of the word *father*, what words come to your mind to define what a father is? I'm sure the sum of possible defini- tions is as wide and varied as there are readers of this book. This is one of the challenges of being a father; there aren't standardized human examples, and so the definitions for fatherhood emerge from experience rather than God, who created fatherhood in the first place. Because experience defines fatherhood for most, the image of what a father is has been marred. Through the failure of some fathers, the family unit has been broken down, and many children have been left with the concept of a father that is completely contradictory to God's original intent. As a result, many mothers are left trying to pick up the pieces in the family and play the role of both mother and father, which further com- plicates the picture. For some children, their mother is the only "father" they have ever known.

The roles of mother and father in the home are distinct because of what each declares to us about God's nature. God has both fathering and mothering qualities. In gen- eral mothers are teachers, comforters, caretakers, and nurturers—pictures of God's instruction and comfort in our lives. Fathers, on the other hand, are protectors, providers, and encouragers—emblems of the Lord's care and encouragement for us.

It's critical for parents to recognize that being a parent isn't simply about taking care of the natural needs of their children; it's also declaring to them through our actions and words what the eternal Father is like. For this to happen, we must know Him ourselves.

Our Example Matters

As a child growing up, my dad had a corporate sales job that required him to travel extensively. He was as involved as he could be in our lives, but often he would have to travel two to three weeks out of a month. We never went without because my dad was great provider, but his work required him to be away from us often.

Growing up, I never thought of my dad as distant or absent; it was just how things were. Years later, though, I realized my image of God was formed by my dad's absence in our home. I assumed God was distant and absent at times from my life. I knew He would ultimately provide for me, just as my earthly dad did, but I wasn't convinced that He wanted to interact with me in the day to day.

When I began to realize the Father is not far off or aloof from me, it radically changed my understanding of God and deeply impacted my approach toward my own children. I recognized that my actions toward my kids would leave an imprint upon their hearts and provide them with the initial way they would picture the Father. I decided as a young father that I wanted to know God and, in turn, to portray Him to my kids in a manner that would help them relate to Him rightly.

As a result, rather than lead my family according to my preferences, I realized my role in the family is to declare the knowledge of God to my kids through my life and actions. This required me to come to know God's love and affection for me and in every circumstance to offer my children a glimpse of God's great love and leadership. This has proven to be a difficult path but an incredibly worthwhile one when it comes to the formation of my children's hearts. I have seen them display incredible confidence that only comes from knowing their father's delight in them.

I'm not saying I've always done it right. On the contrary, at times I've completely misrepresented God. Other times I have not known how to act or what to say. But when I don't know, it's incumbent upon me to seek God that I may know His heart and His ways. It's a brilliant strategy of God that is designed to create intimacy between Himself and us. He puts us in situations that require us to seek Him and come to know Him more. Through our experiential knowledge of Him, we are able then to live our lives knowing His ways and declaring the knowledge of Him to others.

Understand that I am not saying we as earthly parents can perfectly depict the heavenly Father. At our best, we are all broken, fallen, frail representations of who God is. But if we come to know His love for us, we can hopefully model for our kids a right image of God.

My children understand that my role as their dad is to love, care for, and instruct them. They also understand I'm a portrayal of God the Father to them. We've talked about this truth, and it's become very meaningful to them in their walk with the Lord. They understand that no matter how close we are, no matter how good our relationship is, no matter how much I adore them, it is only a small glimpse of the Father's love for them. And they understand that when I blow it, lose my temper, get impatient, or make a bad choice, I am acting nothing like the eternal Father. It brings incredible accountability to you as a parent when you and your children understand that you are supposed to offer them a picture of the Father. When you mess up, it's obvious to everyone—your kids and your spouse—that you are not acting like the One you are supposed to be portraying. This recognition requires you to be humble and ask for forgiveness often.

As a father, this has been an incredible compass for me as I have endeavored to love and lead my family. For instance, in disciplining my children according to God's ways, I have had to learn His dealings with me in my shortcomings as well as His celebration of me in my victories. Then, by His grace, I attempt to offer the same kind of love to my children that God has offered to me.

A Love That Surpasses Shortcomings

I have a much better grasp on how to approach circumstances when our children have fallen short because I'm aware of how the Father has handled me in my own shortcomings. When I make an honest mistake, the Father encourages and affirms me—He doesn't chide me. He's never angry or frustrated with me in my simple errors. Therefore, when dealing with my children, I try to encourage and affirm them rather than get irritated or frustrated when they make an honest mistake. If I do get agitated toward them, I know I'm not acting as the eternal Father acts, and I need to consider His kindness toward me in my weakness and offer that same kindness to my kids.

Affirming and learning to enjoy my children in their shortcomings has created an incredible bond between us. They know that when they fail, I am for them; I'm not going to condemn them. This has cultivated real confidence in their hearts toward me and toward the Lord.

It is imperative that parents be the safest people for their kids to be with. When your child knows he can fail with you and not lose your affection, it creates a powerful and enduring bond between the two of you. This is a massive truth that parents must understand: God is not frustrated or agitated with you when you make a mistake. He still enjoys you in your weaknesses and shortcomings. And we must give that same grace and love to our children.

The other day I was eating lunch with my youngest son and my two-year-old daughter. (After three boys, the Lord blessed us with a baby girl, and she is all that you'd imagine a little girl with three older brothers to be: the center of attention and everybody's princess.) On this particular day my daughter finished first, so we let her get down out of her chair to wander the kitchen as we finished eating. As I scraped together the last bites of my meal, my son, with an excited giggly gasp, exclaimed, "Riah, no!"

I looked up to see my daughter with cheeks packed to the brim. Somehow she had acquired a mouthful of grapes. It was odd because we didn't have grapes for lunch, and there weren't grapes anywhere in sight.

My son continued, "I can't believe it. My baby sister is a raccoon!"

I replied, "What do you mean?"

He effused with glee, "She got them from the garbage!" That's right. My baby girl had dug into the garbage to find a cluster of moldy grapes and packed her cheeks with the tainted fruit. She looked like a chipmunk preparing for winter.

Trying not to bust out laughing, I quickly put my hand in front of her mouth and invited her to spit them out. She willingly deposited them into my palm and then smiled a mischievous smile. The whole scene, along with my son's commentary, was like something from a sitcom.

As I reflected on Riah's foraging escapade, I realized my reaction wasn't one of disgust or frustration. In fact, though the old grapes were repulsive, my only response was delight. My daughter's poor choice in no way hindered my enjoyment of her; in fact, it heightened it.

I realized that when we make mistakes, we often imagine the eternal Father to be frustrated with us because of our inadvertent poor choices. I'm not particularly talking about sin right now—I'll touch on that in a moment. I am talking about when you make an honest mistake because of a bad decision. When we make mistakes, we imagine the Father to have His arms folded, tapping His foot with a sour scowl on His face, frustrated because we are so dumb.

He's not like that. He knows our frame. He knows we are frail and weak, limited in our perspective and ability. He isn't offended or angered by our mistakes; instead, He enjoys us even in the midst of them. When we decide foraging for mildewed fruit from the trash is a good idea, His response isn't agitation; instead, it's affirmation and instruction.

Don't get me wrong. God doesn't want us to eat the "moldy fruit" of our poor decisions. But He isn't as put off by our poor choices as we might imagine. Our honest mistakes don't irk Him a bit. When we err, He affirms us, all the while enjoying us and instructing us in a better way if we'll listen. The entire time He is smiling, delighted and enjoying us.

We must come to grips with the fact that as humans, you and I are very limited in our perspective and understanding. The most astute among us is actually very dim. God knows this and doesn't treat us as if we should know better when we make a mistake. More often, He treats us just like my little raccoon foraging for some moldy grapes.

God is wonderfully gracious with us in our honest mistakes *and* He is wonderfully gracious with us when we directly disobey. There is a great difference between the two, but God remains consistent in both. Too often we imagine God to be angry with us when we sin. Instead, His attitude toward our sin isn't primarily anger, but rather firm, unyielding love. When we sin or disobey, He corrects us, always desiring to restore unbroken fellowship and intimacy. He is not the father who "flies off the handle" when we do something wrong. Instead, He is ever faithful and persistent, drawing and calling us to repentance.

Remember the story of the prodigal son (Luke 15:11–32)? The most incredible part of that story to me is that the father runs to his son. He doesn't stand on the porch with arms folded, scowling in displeasure. Instead, at the first sight of his son, the father runs to him. Do you know the Father who runs to you in your sin? Do you know the Father who still loves you when you fail?

The Father's attitude toward us when we sin instructs our hearts on how we are to handle our children when they rebel. My wife and I decided early on as parents that we would discipline disobedience, not honest mistakes. And in every instance of discipline, we have endeavored to discipline in love rather than in anger or agitation. The Father always sows correction in our lives with peace and unyielding love, never anger, and we are to do the same (Heb. 12:5–11). We made it a value in our home, then, to discipline our children when they disobeyed, but only in peace and love, never in anger for the sole purpose to punish. Discipline is to be redemptive, because the Father's discipline in our lives is always geared toward redemption.

This has required us to be very consistent and communicative in our discipline with our kids. We never leave them wondering what their offense was. And we never leave them wondering if Mommy and Daddy love them. We have made it clear that because we love them, we cannot allow them to continue in rebellion and disobedience. The pain they will feel momentarily from discipline is nothing compared to the lifetime of pain and eternal consequences they would experience from living in rebellion and disobedience.

Misunderstanding God's purposes in discipline often alienates people from God. They don't understand His motives and therefore imagine His correction to be rejection. God only disciplines those whom He loves. He never disciplines out of anger and never in order to reject His children. He always disciplines to restore fellowship. This is His way with us, and it also needs to be our way with our kids. Whether they are older or younger, we should always discipline in love and peace with the intent to bring them back into fellowship with us. Often parents miss an incredible opportunity to instruct the hearts of their children by disciplining them out of anger or neglecting discipline altogether. Neither approach rightly portrays the heart of God. He is the Father who doesn't leave us to ourselves when we sin but convicts us in order to restore us, all for love.

With this in mind, I want to offer an approach to discipline that can be a great portrayal of God's heart toward your kids.

An Approach to Discipline

There are multiple ways to administer discipline: spanking, taking away privileges, time out, adding extra chores, etc. Whatever route you choose, it's important to administer the discipline in a manner that is consistent with the Father's heart. As I said before, it's important to discipline rebellion and disobedience, but never honest mistakes.

When our kids deliberately disobey, we use the rod of correction as the Scripture prescribes (Prov. 22:15; 23:13–14; 29:15). For us the rod is a six-inch wooden spoon. It's amazing how a few licks with a little wooden spoon applied to a child's hinder parts can help produce redemptive and powerful results.

I often see parents who discipline their children regularly but still struggle with their children's behavior even after they discipline them. I am convinced that for discipline to have its proper effect, it has to be sown the way the Father intended. Here are a few guidelines that can help you to convey the Father's heart to your children when you have to discipline them. These guidelines will work for whatever mode of discipline you choose, but they are written with the rod of correction in mind.

1. In all discipline it's important to never threaten without follow through. If you threaten and threaten and never act on your discipline, your children will be trained to believe you don't keep your word and that there are no real consequences for their rebellion. They will, in turn, believe God handles them the same way—that He does not follow through with consequences for sin. It's critically important to be consistent.

2. Before you apply any discipline, set clear expectations for behavior. When your child crosses the line, a warning may be in order first. If they persist, you must follow through with discipline or they will lose respect for you and ultimately God.

3. If you are going to discipline your child, the consequence must be severe enough to cause them to rethink their actions the next time they are posed with the same situation. When disciplining our children, we have found that in order for the discipline to be a deterrent to rebellion, it must be something they do not want to have happen again.

4. Don't flippantly fly off the handle. This response is not representative of the Father's heart and can do much more harm than good. Instead, when your child crosses the line, stop what you are doing and tell them their offense and that they will be getting disciplined as a result. If you use the rod,

take your child to a private place to discuss and administer the discipline.

5. Explain to your child what he has done wrong. Make sure he understands what his infraction is. If your child doesn't understand why he is getting disciplined, it can create fear and distrust in his heart toward you.

6. The more you make of the event, the less often you will have to do it. We have found that consistent, firm discipline, sown in love, has produced in our kids a desire for righteousness at a young age and that as they have grown older, we have not had to discipline them nearly as often.

7. After you are finished administering the discipline, hold your child close. Ask them if they understand why they got disciplined, and offer them the opportunity to express their sorrow for their disobedience. Hold them close until they are once again secure in your love.

8. Once the event is over, it's over. Your child can go right back to playing, eating, or whatever it is they were doing beforehand. Just as with the Lord, when we repent, He no longer keeps a record of our wrongs. Parents often hurt their children by shaming them for past offenses. Use discipline as a means to bring closure to the offense; this will free your child's heart and allow him to move beyond his disobedience.

Every time the Lord has corrected my rebellion, He has always done it with a firm hand of love. He has never left me wondering whether He loved me. At times it has been momentarily painful as I realized the consequences of my sinful actions. But in the end, His corrections have yielded an intense desire in my heart for righteousness and compelled me to love Him even more. This is how our disciplinary actions should affect our children. Much is gained in the lives of our kids when we discipline them through the lens of the knowledge of God.

Parenting, as an institution that declares the knowledge of God, is unique from all other institutions in life because, as parents, we are the primary authors of the image of God in the hearts of our children. We actually participate in the formation of their ideas about God through our words and deeds. What an incredible honor, that God would invite us to know Him and portray Him this way, forever sculpting His image for our kids! Because of this incredible honor, it is essential that we understand this institution and the power it has in forming the knowledge of God in our children's hearts. Every day we are telling our kids something about God. This is why we must come to know God as a Father and engage Him intimately in parenting. The glory of parenting is that we have been given the honor of participating with God to expound the knowledge of Him for our children. How does this alter your approach to parenting? What is the image of God that you are offering your children? I want to encourage you to seek God out as the caring, loving Father that you may portray to your kids a right knowledge of Him.

PART IV

GOD AND MONEY

CHAPTER 12

WHO IS GOD IN FINANCES?

I N ADDITION TO being a Bridegroom and a Father, God is a businessman. Jesus used many parables to depict God as such. He is seen as a merchant (Matt. 13:45), a landowner (Matt. 20:1), a manager (Matt. 25:14), a farmer (Mark 12:1), and a gardener (John 15). Each parable has a specific truth to convey about the kingdom and the ways of God. In a broader sense, each parable portrays God as a workman managing a workforce and budgeting finances.

What does this tell us about God? The obvious answer is first that He is a master craftsman (Prov. 8:30) who loves to work. Think about everything He has made. He worked to form all of creation. He is continually working to form and fashion men's hearts. He is a dedicated and faithful worker. He doesn't work by the sweat of His brow as we do; nonetheless, He is always at work within the affairs of men.

Who God is as a worker speaks to us of the function we are called to fulfill in this life as workers too. Whether we work in the corporate world, as students, as homemakers, or as full-time ministers, all of us are commissioned to work. Some people think that work was part of the curse from Adam's fall. However, work was not the curse—the curse was the stress and strain that would ensue because of sin. Work was present before the fall. God gave Adam several jobs before sin was ever present in the earth: cultivating the garden, naming the animals, and multiplying and populating the earth.

When we work, we connect with a facet of God's nature as the glad worker who does all things well. He loves to create and work, and thus when we work, we find something in our image-bearing nature come alive. There's a special sense of accomplishment we feel when we produce something through work.

We will investigate this idea much further later on. For our purposes in this chapter I want to focus on the reward for work and examine what it testifies about God's nature and character.

Why Money?

There is a reward for labor. All work has a produce. The produce in itself is a reward, but there is also a monetary reward or payment for work. We call it a wage. It's easy to see that work declares the knowledge of God, but in the kingdom of God, don't we receive everything freely by grace? This begs the questions: Are wages OK for us to receive? How are we to regard them? Since money is supposed to declare the knowledge of God, why not have a society without currency where people work and are rewarded out of good will rather than performance? Maybe this kind of system would communicate the knowledge of God more accurately than a monetary system based on accomplishment. "After all, isn't money the root of all evil?" some might ask.

Well, actually, no. The passage actually says the *"love of money"* is the root of all evil (1 Tim. 6:10, emphasis added). Money itself is neither good nor bad. It is, however, incredibly purposeful in declaring the knowledge of God and the ways of His kingdom.

Does it surprise you to hear that? Let me explain.

Money has a twofold purpose. As a reward for work, it is a picture of what Jesus called the "true riches." And it's also a tool God uses to establish His kingdom by bringing us into intimacy with Himself. We'll spend the rest of this chapter investigating this twofold purpose for finances. First, let's take a look at finances as a picture of the true riches, rewards in the kingdom of God.

True Riches

There are multiple references in the Scriptures to eternal rewards. In fact, many times when Jesus motivates us to righteousness, He uses the promise of eternal rewards as inspiration. In one place, for example, He says, "Therefore if you have not been faithful in the unrighteous mammon, who will commit to your trust the true riches?" (Luke 16:11). He's referring here to faithfulness in earthly money as a requisite for receiving eternal rewards.

Our problem is that we have a very dim view of eternal rewards, and so we don't connect to the concept very well. We tend to be dim about rewards because we don't comprehend God's ways. Most of the time when we talk about eternity, we picture an ethereal realm with no tactile reality. We imagine a cloudy, wispy place that lasts a long time but isn't very exciting. Many Christians actually think of heaven as boring.

Rather than being boring, the polar opposite is true. The age to come will find us caught up in the most exhilarating of circumstances. Paul explained that God's plan for the coming age is to unite heaven and earth together under the leadership of Jesus: "And he made known to us the mystery of his will according to his good pleasure, which he purposed in Christ, to be put into effect when the times will have reached their fulfillment—to bring all things in heaven and on earth together under one head, even Christ" (Eph. 1:9–10, NIV). Do you realize heaven and earth will be joined together with Jesus as the leader over all? This truth is astounding. As believers, this is where we are all headed. The entire planet will come under the leadership of Jesus, and all "the earth will be filled with the knowledge of the glory of the LORD, as the waters cover the sea" (Hab. 2:14).

This joining of heaven and earth will happen at the return of the Lord, when the kingdoms of this world fully come under Jesus's leadership (Rev. 11:15). The next age will begin with the saints from this age ruling with Jesus on the earth (Rev. 2:26-27; 5:10; 20:4). And there will be tangible continuity between this age and the next. National governments, economic systems, agricultural processes—these will all remain intact. Jesus will rule the nations of the earth bodily from Jerusalem, and we His saints will work with Him in His kingdom (Isa. 60:5–22; Ps. 2:6–12; Dan. 7:13–14). The Bible paints a picture of participation and partnership between God and man for ages to come.

This picture is far different from what may be in our minds regarding the age to come. Again, the most common depiction of that age includes saints floating around in some ethereal realm without any care or responsibility. This idea is not even close to what the Bible describes. In the age to come believers will partner with Jesus in His leadership of the nations. How fascinating is that?

When it comes to rewards, most believers are solely focused on the rewards they will receive in this age. This is an incredibly shortsighted view. The Scriptures outline many rewards promised to believers, the vast majority of which will not be realized until the age to come—not in this age. The fact is, how we spend our lives in this age determines what rewards we receive in the next. We are promised seventy to eighty years in this age, but in the next age all the redeemed will live on the earth for one thousand years. And that doesn't even take into account all of eternity that will follow those thousand years!

If you live only seventy to eighty years in this age but are going to live a thousand in the next, which age should you spend most of your energy investing in? We have to get our minds around the fact that there are *ages* to come (Eph. 2:7). This current age is at best an internship for how we will spend the next ages. It's imperative, then, that we live in a way right now that makes sense for the coming ages.

And now we come back to the question of money. Heaven's reward system in the coming ages is the basis for the wages we receive from our jobs in this age. In other words, your job right now, which pays you a wage, declares a colossal truth. It speaks of the eternal wages you will receive as a result of how you serve the Lord in this age.

Our role in the next age is determined by how we live in this age. We will have specific assignments, or jobs, in the next age that are being determined right now by how we live here. This is what Jesus described in the parable of the minas (Luke 19:12–27). A mina was an ancient weight that determined a portion of silver. One mina would be equivalent to approximately seven hundred fifty dollars in today's currency. The first servant in the parable used the finances he was given to produce ten times more. As a result, the lord rewarded him with ten cities. The next servant multiplied his lord's initial investment by a factor of five. As a result, the lord awarded him with five cities. The final servant did not use the lord's investment at all, and instead of offering a return to his master, he had nothing to show for what he had been given. In return, even what he had been given was taken from him.

This parable portrays a vital truth: the way we steward the Lord's investment in our lives now determines the role we will have in the kingdom when the Lord returns. Our faithfulness now is going to qualify us or disqualify us for service in the next age.

Our jobs today are a picture of this vitally important truth. Wages, bonuses, promotions, and raises all speak to us of the way the Lord will reckon our service to Him in this age and the role He will assign to us in the next. The entire institution of work with wages and rewards is actually a declaration of how God will assess and reward us in the age to come. It really is true that whoever is faithful in this age over what the Lord has entrusted will be made faithful over much in the next age. And whoever is unfaithful over what the Lord has entrusted in this age will not receive the Lord's commendation in the next age (Luke 19:17, 19, 24–26; Matt. 25:21, 23, 28–29).

The Scriptures make it clear that there are real rewards for the saints. These rewards, while spiritual, will also be very tangible. Money as a reward for work in this age is a picture of the rewards we will receive in the next age. Jesus even went as far as to say that the way that we handle money in this age, whether we handle it faithfully or not, determines whether or not God will entrust to us the true riches in the age to come (Luke 16:11).

In this age the Lord entrusts us as stewards. And when the Lord returns, He will review our stewardship and reward us according to our faithfulness. Our daily jobs and monetary incomes are designed to speak to us every single day of this eternal reality: we will all stand before the living God, give an account of our faithfulness to Him in this life, and receive what is due us according to our works while we lived on the earth (2 Cor. 5:10). Paul explained that the rewards saints receive at the judgment will differ from person to person and are determined by the way they lived in this age (1 Cor. 15:41–44). The Lord has given us the institution of work as a continual testimony of this essential truth.

With this in mind, let's consider the idea of ownership and what it speaks to us about God.

Ownership or Stewardship?

Imagine you receive a five-thousand-dollar check in the mail from an old family friend who said they wanted to "bless" you. After you finished jumping for joy, how would you spend the money? Would you buy something you've had your eye on for a while? Save some? Give some? Like most people, you'd probably do a little of each. The decision probably wouldn't require much thought.

Now imagine a different scenario. Instead of receiving a check from a friend, imagine an angel appears to you and hands you a stack of fifty one-hundred-dollar bills. After you scraped yourself up off the floor, how would you go about handling this money? Would you go about it differently than the money you received from the friend?

You would probably pray and make completely sure you knew exactly what God wanted you to do with that money before you even thought about spending it, right?

Why is there a difference between how we would handle the money in the first example versus the second? Undoubtedly because we don't think of a check from a friend in the same way we would think of a stack of "holy hundreds" from an angel. The question is: Are they any different? Is the money from a friend our money, while the money from an angel is God's money? Is there really any difference between the two?

The reason we think differently about these two examples is because we don't have a clear picture of our responsibility in regard to stewardship, and we lack a biblical mentality of ownership. The concepts of stewardship and ownership speak much to us about God's nature. But before we can comprehend God in these institutions, we must have a biblical paradigm of them.

Think for a minute about all the things that are yours. Do you own a car, a house, a computer? What about clothes, furniture, a television? How long is the list of stuff you own? How did you acquire these things? Did you buy them? Were they gifts? Did you work for them?

This may surprise you, but everything on your list isn't actually yours. In fact, in the kingdom of God, we are not owners of anything we possess. We are stewards. Through multiple verses God makes it clear He is the one who owns all the goods that exist in creation:

> The earth is the LORD's, and all its fullness.
>
> —PSALM 24:1

The silver is Mine, and the gold is Mine.

—HAGGAI 2:8

For every beast of the forest is Mine, and the cattle on a thousand hills. I know all the birds of the mountains, and the wild beasts of the field are Mine.

—PSALM 50:10–11

For all that is in heaven and earth is Yours.

—1 CHRONICLES 29:11–12

Though the Scriptures are clear that God owns everything, including "our" money and goods, many believers only view 10 percent of their income as belonging to the Lord. Some go a little further and think of the tithe plus an additional "offering" as what belongs to God. But who thinks that *all* of their possessions are the Lord's? Believers tend to think that the 10–20 percent they give is the Lord's, while the remaining 80–90 percent is theirs to spend as they will. They think giving the tithe and offering is a spiritual decision, while spending the remainder is a natural decision—not necessarily spiritual.

Most modern teachings on stewardship encourage believers to try to spend the remainder in a "responsible" way so they can be considered a "good steward." Many Christians acknowledge they are supposed to be good stewards, but they have a limited understanding of what stewardship really is. Most people believe stewardship boils down to being financially responsible or handling money with wisdom.

However, the biblical examples of stewardship do not merely portray someone who manages their goods responsibly. Instead, the Bible portrays a steward as a *servant* who manages *someone else's* goods and finances in a way that pleases the owner (Matt. 25:14–30; Luke 16:1–10). The biblical mentality of stewardship is actually this: "Nothing I own is mine; everything I have belongs to the Lord."

How few of us have this paradigm, and how few of us manage our finances based on the truth that we own nothing—that we are merely stewards for God! He is the owner of 100 percent of all we possess. When we believe anything we have is our own, we are completely out of touch with what the Bible teaches about ownership and stewardship.

The implications of understanding the truth of stewardship should radically change our approach to our money. I have heard many teachers and preachers say, "It's OK to have things as long as things don't have you." The biblical perspective is that you actually have *nothing*, because ownership is ultimately the Lord's, not yours. There is a massive difference between seeing yourself as the owner instead of seeing the Lord as the owner and you as the steward.

For instance, when it comes to giving, if you think of yourself as the owner, you might think a godly approach to giving is to give *your* finances anytime God asks you. That seems good at a glance, but a proper understanding of stewardship is seeing everything you have as belonging to God. Since it's all His, He can tell you to give away or keep as much of it as He wants. The goods have always been His; they've never been yours. Therefore, what you have, you have received from His hand, and He can direct you how to manage all of them as He wishes.

There is incredible liberty in this mentality. Furthermore, the proper mentality of stewardship is critical to our relationship with the Lord. Jesus spoke specifically about the concept of ownership in regard to our discipleship. He said if we claim that we own anything ourselves, we cannot be His disciples: "So then, none of you can be My disciple *who does not give up all his own possessions*" (Luke 14:33, NAS, emphasis added). That definitely raises the stakes on stewardship as it relates to our relationship with the Lord, doesn't it?

This understanding of stewardship and ownership offers us an amazing picture of who God is. Why does God give us this model of stewardship instead of allowing us to be owners? Is He trying to withhold from us in some way? Doesn't He want to give us things?

God is not withholding from us in any way. He promises to give the redeemed all things (Rom. 8:32; Rev. 21:7). Once again He is declaring of Himself through it. The real question we have to ask is, "How does this model of stewardship declare the knowledge of God?"

Though Jesus is coequal and coexistent with the Father, the Scriptures are clear that He has humbled Himself and taken a subservient position within the Godhead. Paul explains that though Jesus existed in the form of God, He humbled Himself and took on the form of a servant (Phil. 2:6–7). As a Son and a servant on the earth, Jesus modeled perfect humility in submission to the Father's will, even to the extent that He only said what the Father told Him to say and only did what the Father showed Him to do (John 5:19, 30). The crowning moment of Jesus's amazing humility was in the garden, when as a man He submitted His will to the Father and humbled Himself to the point of death.

That is not the final act of His humility, though. The Scriptures tell us that Jesus will rule the age to come by asking the Father to release and implement *His will* on the earth (Ps. 2:7–8). In other words, Jesus will govern the nations through prayer, preferring the Father's plan over His own—the ultimate act of humility.

What's more, after every enemy has been defeated, when sin and death are finally destroyed and everything under creation is fully subject to Jesus, He will perform one final act of incredible humility, revealing His role in creation. He will give everything back to the Father, that the Father may "be all in all" (1 Cor. 15:25–28).

It's an incredible thought, but it's true: Jesus Christ as the second person of the Trinity is acting as a steward of all that the Father owns, and when everything is fully under His authority, He will hand everything back to the Father. He has been given all authority in heaven and earth now, but a day is coming when that authority will be fully manifest over all creation. Once the full extent of His authority is realized, He will once again humble Himself and deliver it all back to the Father.

Our role as stewards, therefore, is simply a picture of Jesus's own humility and stewardship in managing all that the Father owns. He is the model for stewardship, and we, as stewards of everything the Father has given us, are a picture of Jesus. A proper understanding of stewardship enables our hearts to serve God with freedom and humility and find Jesus in the midst of it all.

Money as a Tool for Intimacy

This brings us to the second key purpose for money: as a tool God uses to bring us into intimacy with Himself. The principles Jesus covers in Matthew 6:19–21 lay the foundation:

> Do not store up for yourselves treasures on earth, where moth and rust destroy, and where thieves break in and steal. But store up for yourselves treasures in heaven, where moth and rust do not destroy, and where thieves do not break in and steal. For *where your treasure is, there your heart will be also.*
>
> —MATTHEW 6:19–21, NIV, EMPHASIS ADDED

Jesus's first admonishment in this passage is to not focus your heart on gaining earthly treasures. Earthly treasures, He says, are temporal, frail, and subject to decay and loss. He then introduces the idea of heavenly treasures that have eternal value and are not subject to loss or decay. The key is the posture of the heart. Wherever you put your treasure, your heart will follow. In other words, what you value most will gain your affections. This means you can use money to bring your heart closer to God. The inverse is also true—you can use money in a way that causes your heart to become distant from God.

Jesus also makes the point that you can convert earthly money into heavenly treasure by investing it in things that have eternal impact rather than spending it on things that have only temporal value. If a man spends money primarily on temporal treasures, not only will he have no heavenly treasures, but also his heart will be disconnected from God, anchored to his earthly treasures. The way he spends money, then, identifies his heart posture and true allegiance. It is as Jesus goes on to say in Matthew 6:24, "No one can serve two masters....You cannot serve both God and Money" (NIV).

We are supposed to steward money, not serve it. The

Lord makes it clear that when we set our hearts on using money to gain earthly treasures, instead of us managing money, the money manages us. We actually become its servant rather than the Lord's steward. What an incredible disparity. When money is used properly, it can bring our hearts closer in intimacy to God. When it is used improperly, it can make us its slave and draw our hearts away from God. How important it is to view money in its proper light and use it for the purpose God intended!

How exactly, then, does God use money as a tool for intimacy? Since God owns all the money we have, every financial decision is actually a spiritual decision. Not only is our tithe and offering a spiritual matter, but also so is how we steward all God has given us. God intends that every financial decision we make be the result of a conversation we have with Him. As His steward, we ought to engage with Him to know His heart and desire for the finances He has placed in our hands. Therefore, whether a person has a little or a lot, the management of those funds is a matter of intimacy with God. This is why Jesus said if you are faithful in a little, you will be faithful in a lot. The issue is not the amount that you have to manage. The issue is whether or not you inquire of the Lord to faithfully manage His finances the way He intends.

Some may immediately think that since finances are actually spiritual, the spiritual thing to do is to give it all away. However, that's not necessarily the case. There are scriptures that encourage saving money as well as spending money on your needs (Prov. 13:22; 24:27, Luke 14:28–30). In fact, God commands us to provide for the needs of our own families (1 Tim. 5:8). Of course, there is a great difference between needs and wants, and that's why intimacy with God is so critical. It's possible that

God may lead one person to give everything away while He leads another person to save their money for something in the future. Staying close to God's heart will keep us out of covetousness and flowing in generosity toward others. Ultimately the question is: Have you stayed in communication with the owner of your assets closely enough to know what it is that He desires you to do with them?

Many Americans dream of achieving financial independence. They believe that having few finances makes you a servant to finances and that having an abundance makes you free. However, it's not the amount of finances you have but rather your heart posture toward them that determines whether you serve finances or you serve the Lord. There are many people who have a lot of finances who are serving their finances rather than serving the Lord. They live day in and day out working tirelessly to get more money, in quest of the goal of financial freedom. However, Paul tells us the desire to be rich causes many to fall into temptations and snares that "drown men in destruction" (1 Tim. 6:9).

Though financial independence sounds great, it is actually contrary to Scripture. God does not want us financially independent, He wants us 100 percent financially dependent upon Him. In fact, He wants us dependent upon Him in *every* area of our lives. Dependence upon God cultivates increased intimacy in our hearts. When we are completely dependent upon God, then and only then are we truly free.

Financial freedom, then, should be our goal, not financial independence. When God gives a person a lot of money, I see it as God's invitation to that person to know Him more intimately. If you understand that setting your heart on money can cause you to depart from God and that seeking to be rich can "drown you in destruction" when money comes your way, it should immediately alert you that you need to go to the Lord and find His heart. The greater the amount of wealth a person is entrusted with, the greater the temptation to stray from the Lord. But at the same time, the greater the amount of wealth, the greater is the invitation to come close to His heart. It's not that God wants certain people closer than others; it's simply that He uses finances as a tool to cause us to seek Him. And in our continual leaning on the Lord, He instructs us in His ways and nature and we find the knowledge of God.

When we begin to grasp this concept, we will handle our finances much differently. Rather than thinking, "What do I want to spend my money on?" or "I want to save my money to buy this in the future," our thought process becomes, "God, how do You want me to spend Your money?" and "If I spend money on this, will it move my heart nearer to or farther from You?"

This brings us back to the example of the angel giving us five thousand dollars. What if we treated every penny we ever received as if it were given to us by the hand of God? We would run to Him for every financial decision and find ourselves flowing in intimacy with Him at a much greater level. When we are financially free, finances no longer rule over us, but we are free from their control in intimate obedience to God.

Called to Account as Stewards

An important reminder for us as stewards is that we will all be called to account for how we handled God's money and possessions while we were on the earth. We have a very real appointment with the Lord coming up to review our stewardship at the judgment seat of Christ. Since we will give an account for our stewardship, it's critical that we live in this age with that future appointment in mind. A good question to give us a standard for how to spend money is: "How will I feel about this decision when I am standing before the judgment seat?" Many things that we feel we "just *have* to get" right now will not seem like such a wise investment when we are standing face-to-face with Jesus. Matthew Henry said, "It ought to be the business every day to prepare for our final day."[1] It's incredibly important that we recognize all that we do now will be recalled and reflected to us in eternity.

A practical way we can help ensure that review will be favorable is to plan, by the leading of the Lord, how to spend and manage money on a weekly and monthly basis. A Spirit-led plan for spending finances can help us stay out of frivolous spending and focus on our approach to stewardship.

Many Christians believe they do not have enough income to go through the hassle of using a budget. This mentality is exactly the opposite of what the Bible teaches. We must stop using a small income as an excuse for being lazy in our stewardship. The way in which you use the money you have will impact you *for the rest of eternity.* This truth must become real to us and govern the way we steward our finances.

Think of it this way. If you were looking for a steward to hire, would you hire a person with no plan? Can you imagine interviewing a money manager and asking him how he planned to manage the finances you invest with him, only to hear he has no real plan but would simply buy stocks on a whim, as it seemed good to him in the moment? You would never hire someone with no plan. What if you did find a money manager with a plan— would you want his plan to be based on his own wants and desires or on your goals and objectives?

As stewards, we must come to grips with the fact that we are managers of God's money. That everything we own is ultimately His. That our stewardship is a picture of Jesus's stewardship in the Father's kingdom and that money is a tool God uses to train our hearts in obedience and draw us near in intimacy.

CHAPTER 13

GENEROSITY, CONTENTMENT, AND TRUE RICHES

Quite a gulf exists in Christian teachings on finances. On the one hand are teachers who emphasize God's desire to make believers rich. They quote verses such as Deuteronomy 8:18—"It is He who gives you the power to get wealth"—often with the exact excerpt I have used. People walk away from this kind of teaching believing God wants everyone rich. I remember as a young believer hearing prosperity messages that emphasized verses like this one and walking away convinced God wanted to make everyone a millionaire.

Unfortunately such teachings tend to ignore the context of the verse and ultimately change the meaning of what the Bible teaches. For instance, the previous verses in Deuteronomy 8 are admonitions to the nation of Israel not to turn away from the Lord when they have prospered financially. Verse 18 is the punch line of the admonition— because it's the Lord who has given you the wealth, all for the purpose of establishing the covenant He promised to Abraham. When read in context, the verse is quite different from the unilateral idea that God just wants to make everyone a millionaire.

On the other end of the spectrum are teachers who

emphasize verses such as James 5:1, which appears to depict the wealthy as sinners: "Now listen, you rich people, weep and wail because of the misery that is coming upon you" (NIV). A casual reading of this verse may lead us to believe that God is opposed to believers possessing wealth in this age. But here again, the context instructs us in the truth. The Lord is prophesying through James to a specific group of wealthy people who will live at the end of the age and deal treacherously with their workers by not paying them the wages they have been promised. Teachers who leave this context out of their teaching give people the impression that God never gives anyone temporal wealth and that if someone does gain wealth, it should be their ambition to give it all away as soon as possible because possessing wealth is sin and the righteous would never do such a thing.

Each of these differing views is incomplete and misleading. As a result, people end up with wrong perceptions about God. The error comes in thinking of man as the main point in the question of finances. Having a man-centered view of anything will give us a twisted picture of what that thing is really about.

As we've discussed throughout this book, God is always declaring Himself through the various institutions of life. Finances are no different. We must have a God-centered view of finances if we are to understand God's purposes for them and use them properly in our lives.

So how are we to approach finances? What is God's plan for our financial supply? Does He want us to be exceedingly wealthy, or is it His desire for us to be poor so that we may be holy?

First, let's address the mentality that God desires everyone to be exceedingly wealthy. We will call this a "prosperity mentality." In this view, wealth is depicted as the capstone of spiritual blessing. If a believer is wealthy, it is assumed he or she has received God's blessing. If people aren't wealthy, they are seen as not having had enough faith to receive God's blessing. Monetary wealth is likened to spiritual maturity and believed to be the evidence of faith and spirituality. Believers therefore seek earthly prosperity because they equate it to spiritual prosperity.

This mentality flies in the face of Scripture's teaching because seeking to get rich is strongly warned against in the Bible. For instance:

> A faithful man will be richly blessed, but *one eager to get rich* will not go unpunished.
> —PROVERBS 28:20, NIV, EMPHASIS ADDED

The Hebrew word translated "go unpunished" here gives the sense of the person eager to get rich not being clean or blameless. In other words, being eager to get rich will likely lead you into compromise that will corrupt you.

Furthermore, Paul admonishes believers to flee from the pursuit and love of money and encourages them instead to pursue righteousness:

> People who want to get rich fall into temptation and a trap and into many foolish and harmful desires that plunge men into ruin and destruction. For the love of money is a root of all kinds of evil. Some people, eager for money, have wandered from the faith and pierced themselves with many griefs. But you, man of God, flee from all this, and pursue righteousness.
> —1 TIMOTHY 6:9–11, NIV

Notice that Paul does not say, "*Some* who want to get rich fall into temptation…" Instead He says, "*People* who want to get rich.*" This means everyone who desires to get rich.

We can easily acknowledge that the love of money is evil, but can we acknowledge that the desire to get rich is also evil? Who has *not* wanted to get rich? How different this perspective is from so many of the prosperity teachings that lead people to believe wealth is to be sought after as a sign of the blessing of the Lord!

With these things so explicitly detailed in Scripture, the question then becomes: Is God against His people having wealth? Does He desire that His people be poor to maintain a standard of holiness?

Let's take a look at the opposing view offered by biblical teachers. We will call this the "poverty mentality." The poverty mentality sees possessions as evil and anyone who has lots of possessions is likely in sin. If God does give finances, the "spiritual" thing to do is to give them away as fast as possible so not to be stained by unrighteousness.

This mentality, just like the prosperity mentality, is in opposition to the clear teachings of Scripture. For instance, David, whom God described as "a man after His own heart" (1 Sam. 13:14), had personal wealth that would have exceeded a billion dollars by today's standards. How could he who was after God's own heart have had all this money if having lots of money is sinful? Abraham, Solomon, Jacob, Job, and many other key biblical figures were greatly increased in material possession—and by the Lord's own doing.

Next, consider this passage from Proverbs:

> The blessing of the Lord brings wealth, and he
> adds no trouble to it.
> —Proverbs 10:22, niv

The writer of Proverbs is clear that the Lord is the one who brings wealth to His people and that when it is the Lord's doing, it is never accompanied by calamity. Though the warnings are clear that if one seeks wealth it will bring a snare, it is also clear that God gives His people material wealth—and that when God releases the prosperity, it is trouble-free.

Since it's evident that God gives wealth to people, but it is also clear that we should not seek material possessions, how then should we posture our hearts in regard to finances? Jesus's teaching adds an additional consideration that brings clarity to the chief mentality we should have toward money:

> Then he said to them, "Watch out! *Be on your guard against all kinds of greed*; a man's life does not consist in the abundance of his possessions."
> —Luke 12:15, niv, emphasis added

Jesus's warning is a plumb line that helps us to gauge our hearts in regard to material possessions. His explicit warning is against greed of every kind. Many equate wealth with greed, but the issue of greed is found in the reach of the heart, not the size of the bank account. Having a lot of finances in no way makes one greedy. There are just as many greedy people who live in poverty as there are who live in extravagance. At the same time many who possess lots of material wealth live their lives greedily, pursuing as much as they can with very little thought of giving.

Comparing Jesus's warning with other scriptural teachings on finances brings us to a simple definition of greed: living for the pursuit of money and temporal wealth.

As stewards, we are to pursue God rather than money and gratefully receive from His hand all that He gives. Whether we receive a little or a lot is not the issue. The issue is a heart of faithfulness to manage all God gives according to His desires. This requires intimacy with God and a heart posture of contentment. If we are to have a biblical paradigm regarding finances, we must allow the Lord to examine our hearts regularly and repent of the desire to get rich. Paul's advice to us is to flee greed at the first sign of it.

Still, the question remains: Is it wrong to be wealthy? Let's further examine Paul's teaching on riches and wealth to more fully develop a biblical paradigm.

> Command *those who are rich* in this present world not to be arrogant nor to put their hope in wealth, which is so uncertain, but to put their hope in God, who richly provides us with everything for our enjoyment. *Command them to do good, to be rich in good deeds, and to be generous and willing to share.* In this way *they will lay up treasure for themselves* as a firm foundation *for the coming age*, so that they may take hold of the life that is truly life.
> —1 TIMOTHY 6:17–19, NIV, EMPHASIS ADDED

Here Paul instructs Timothy what to teach those in the church who are rich in this age. Notice that he does not say that they are ungodly because they are rich. Nor does he instruct them to give away everything and become poor as a means of holiness. Paul identifies God as the one who supplies us with everything we need as well as things beyond our needs, even things for our enjoyment. Paul says to command the rich to be generous, holding on to an eternal perspective. He calls them to recognize that all they have comes from God and He will reward them in the age to come based on how they use what He has given them in this age.

Paul's teachings on generosity raised the bar for the New Testament church. Whereas in the Old Testament the standard was the tithe, in the New Testament the standard for giving is generosity and a willingness to share. The tithe is not canceled out in the New Testament; it is carried over. But instead of tithing being the high bar of giving, it is the low bar. Generosity is the new standard. God calls us to give in a radical way that is in sync with His heart and by the direction of the Holy Spirit. Generosity compels us to not only put our 10 percent in the offering plate but also to be willing to give and share at all times in whatever way the Lord desires. After all, it's His money anyway.

The two differing attitudes, poverty and prosperity, stand in stark opposition to one another and wage war against the knowledge of God in regard to finances. Neither position is actually the biblical mentality. The biblical mentality is found through embracing the proper ideas of stewardship that we discussed in the previous chapter. When we finally agree that everything we have is the Lord's, we then can step into the cure for each of these extreme mentalities: contentment.

Settling Into Contentment

> …men of corrupt mind, who have been robbed
> of the truth and who think that godliness is a
> means to financial gain. But *godliness with con-*
> *tentment is great gain.* For we brought nothing
> into the world, and we can take nothing out of it.
> But *if we have food and clothing, we will be con-*
> *tent with that.*
> —1 Timothy 6:5–8, niv, emphasis added

Paul prefaces his comments to Timothy with the "contentment mentality" each of us as believers is to embrace. He presents contentment as the antidote to greed. His approach may seem radical in our society, but Paul is straightforward that we are to be content with food and clothing. In other words, those goods should be enough to make us content.

How could we be content with so little? Because we know that all we have comes from the Lord and that He is the One who supplies all of our needs. Notice Paul's emphasis on the fact that we have entered this world with nothing and we will exit it with nothing. This is the cornerstone understanding of stewardship: all that we have comes from God and all that He gives is ultimately His.

Paul also teaches:

> I am not saying this because I am in need, for *I*
> *have learned to be content whatever the circum-*
> *stances.* I know what it is to be in need, and I
> know what it is to have plenty. I have learned *the*
> *secret of being content in any and every situa-*
> *tion,* whether well fed or hungry, whether living

in plenty or in want. I can do everything through him who gives me strength.
—Philippians 4:11–13, niv, emphasis added

Notice that he points out contentment as the cure for both the prosperity *and* the poverty mentality. He says in abundance or in great need, the secret to handling all circumstances is contentment. Contentment is simply this: being satisfied with what God supplies, whether it's a lot or a little. When we begin to think, "I would be satisfied if I just had this one more thing…," we have moved out of contentment and are headed toward greed.

Paul says contentment was not something he was born with—he had to *learn* it. The reason this mentality of contentment seems so radical is that we are discontent by nature. Because of sin, we always want more and tend toward greed instead of satisfaction. In America, it's unfortunate, but most have grown to believe they deserve certain things in life. This is an "entitlement mentality." The entitlement mentality wars against contentment and is contradictory to what it means to be a steward. Wherever the entitlement mentality is present in us, we must turn from it and turn to God with grateful hearts for all that He has supplied. We learn to be content in any and all circumstances, by thanking Him for taking care of us and supplying for us, no matter how little or how much we have.

One final admonition from the writer of Hebrews seals the biblical mentality of stewardship with contentment:

Keep your lives free from the love of money and *be content with what you have*, because God has said, "Never will I leave you; never will I forsake you."
—Hebrews 13:5, niv, emphasis added

167

Freedom from the love and pursuit of money is a key to contentment. Rather than focusing on what we *don't* have, we should be content with whatever we *do* have. The reason we can be content is that no matter what we do not have, we *do* have God.

And this brings us to an extremely important idea concerning contentment: *Whatever I have and whatever I do not have, it is infinitely better than what I deserve.* Knowing that we are saved from wrath by the grace of God liberates our heart from discontentment and entitlement and allows us to embrace a stewardship paradigm rooted in a contentment mentality.

Now that we have established God's purposes in money and His plan to use finances as a tool for intimacy, let's consider our final institution that declares the knowledge of God: our jobs.

PART V

GOD AND MISSION

CHAPTER 14

REDEFINING MISSION

THE SCOPE OF the tragedy of the fall of man and his subsequent banishment from the Garden of Eden is inestimable. The repercussions from that time until now have been vast. Not only did sin and death infect and ravage the entire human race, but also mankind lost his intimate relationship with God. When we consider the state of the world today, so much of what has taken place in the earth is as a result of that original treachery. War, murder, rape, and every human atrocity that has ever taken place are linked to that original failure.

Imagine the sense of horror Adam felt the moment he first sensed life drain from his spirit. His stomach dropped as his soul grew cold, all for a mouthful of fruit. While the flavor was still upon his tongue, sin infected his entire being, and everything he perceived was now completely different: pale, wretched, *fallen*. He was created fully alive—spirit, soul, and body—and now that life was distant and gone. Death crept over his mind and constricted all his capacities. Fret, fear, and shame flooded his heart, each one something he'd never experienced before. And with every passing moment, a new fallen emotion gripped him. With every new emotion, he was introduced to a new torment. The bliss of pleasure and freedom were gone. Condemnation ran through him like a flood. His eyes were opened in the most terrible way—a way he'd never dreamed. And then the moment of reckoning came as he "heard the sound of the LORD God walking in the garden in the cool of the day" (Gen. 3:8). Who knows how many times before he'd grown excited at the sound of the Father's footsteps? Every time prior to this one Adam's heart filled with expectancy as the Father drew near. He had shared the heights of sweet intimacy without any barriers with the Father.

But not this time. Now his immediate response was fear.

> Then the LORD God called to Adam and said to Him, "Where are you?"
> —GENESIS 3:9

How those words must have echoed ominously in Adam's ears! *Where are you?* A pit formed in his stomach as he struggled to find the words. Nerve-racked, with a dry mouth, he answered, "I heard your voice in the garden, and I was afraid because I was naked; and I hid myself" (Gen. 3:10).

Until now every time Adam had heard the Father's voice, his heart leapt with delight. This time his heart sank in fear. Instead of feeling affirmed by the Father, he was afraid of Him. Had the Father changed? No. The effects of sin had changed Adam. He was alienated from the One who loved him completely.

Whenever I read the story of the fall, I'm struck by the Father's tenderness toward Adam. Instead of raging against Adam as an enemy, the Father handles him like a child who stepped over the line. Firmly but tenderly the Father questions His son and finds at the root of the sin the invitation of the serpent. After addressing the serpent, the Father disciplines His children.

Of special note is that single question that opens the

dialogue: "Where are you?" This question gives us insight into the Father's ongoing plans toward humanity.

When God created man, He knew there would be a day when humanity would choose to rebel against Him and intimacy would be lost. Adam's sin did not catch the Father by surprise. In a certain way, you could say God had been preparing for this moment forever. When God asked Adam, "Where are you?", it was not because the Father could not find him. The Lord asked the question to communicate two key truths: the reality of Adam's state and the kindness of the Father's intention toward him.

Adam's State

"Where are you, Adam?"

"I don't know where I am. I can't see. I feel horrid. And You sound different, haunting and distorted. I'm scared. I feel sick. The life I had is gone. I don't know what to do or how to get out of here. I don't know where I am...I'm lost!"

That's it. From the moment of the fall, humanity has been lost. This is our state without God: *lost*.

A lost world doesn't know how to live. A lost people look to everything else for life—anything they can to find their way. But the problem remains. Without the light that God gives, we are lost and cannot find our way. Thus, we try to find identity in everything and anything that will promise us life. When our center is not God, we lose perspective and direction. Lost means you don't know where you are and you don't know where to go. In every area of life we are lost without God.

The huge error of lost men is to focus on themselves as their compass. We in the church repeat this same error when we look to ourselves as the center of our lives. But looking to ourselves first keeps us lost. When we look to God as the center, as the reason for life, its relationships, and its institutions, we are found. It's only in the light of God that we can see, understand, and have clarity.

The Father's Intention

From the moment of the fall heaven's action plan has been to recover relationship with humanity. Immediately God rebuked the serpent and declared His intention to redeem man and destroy the enemy through the seed of the woman, Jesus. When God asked Adam, "Where are you?", He had moved from fellowship into search-and-rescue mode. This was God's immediate intention for humanity, and it is God's continuous intention toward humanity today: to seek and save the lost.

God is ever pursuing humanity, and it is in this light that we can see God as the original missionary. His plan has always been to regain intimacy with us. When we comprehend human existence through the lens of God's desire for intimacy, we gain incredible perspective. And this is the big point: it's only in understanding God's mission that we can make sense of our own.

In the church we have made a major mistake by believing the works of the ministry are to be done by the ministers. The works of the ministry are to be done by *all* the saints (Eph. 4:12). Furthermore, we have primarily associated the "works of the ministry" with serving in the local church. I agree that serving in church is part of doing the works of the ministry, but it is not the sole way we engage in ministry.

In addition to serving in church, we are to engage in the works of the ministry by engaging in God's mission toward humanity to seek and save the lost. Getting a paycheck or simply having something to do isn't the main reason we work where we do. The main reason we work in the field that we work is because God is on a mission and He wants us to share that mission with Him in that place. He wants us to engage with Him in reaching the lost.

Are you able to accept that the reason you have a desire to work in a specific field is because there are others in that field that God wants to reach through you? Your interest in your particular occupation comes as a result of God's design and His intention to touch those people in that field through you as a missionary.

We have emphasized our own dreams and desires far too much. We have made our reason for being primarily about ourselves, and in doing so we have completely missed the point that God has dreams and desires too. His dream is to restore the lost intimacy He once shared with humanity. His invitation to you and me is to partner with Him in His dream.

Wherever we are employed, it's our opportunity, our invitation, to engage with God in His mission. The mission is not simply for missionaries or ministers; this mission is for the family of God. The idea that there are clergy and laity is completely foreign to God's intention for the church. He desires that all His people know Him as a missionary and engage with Him in His quest.

Our Identity Is Beloved

In the kingdom of God our identity is not our vocation. In fact, our identity in the kingdom is so highly exalted that there is nothing we can do in this life to improve upon it.

Our earthly job is not our ultimate identity, nor is it our ultimate purpose. Our purpose is far greater than any job we will hold in this age, and our identity is far superior to any career path we choose. If we identify ourselves by our earthly jobs, we greatly diminish the truth of who we are in the kingdom of God. God never intended for any one of us to be identified by our vocation. Whether we are a businessman, a homemaker, or a student, none of these vocations are to be our sole identity. Our true identity is far beyond our natural roles.

Every believer carries one title that trumps all other labels: beloved. Our identity is "one who is cherished and loved by God." There is no higher identity than this. If you don't recognize the exaltation, beauty, and dignity of being the beloved of God, if that is not valuable to you, it is because you do not actually have revelation of this incredible truth. Every possible earthly station is infinitely inferior to the truth of being the beloved of God.

Our Eternal Purpose

Just as with our identity, our purpose is not confined to anything we do in this age. Our purpose is eternal, just as God's purposes are eternal. What that means is that our purpose has far-reaching implications beyond anything that we will accomplish now. Though we have giftings and callings in this life, our ultimate calling is not any job we will perform in this age.

If we imagine that our highest calling is working for God in this age, we greatly belittle our calling. Romans 8:28 says we are "called according to His purpose." Notice this is a singular purpose, not multiple. In other words, there is a singular purpose in the heart of God for you that is far above any other purpose you fulfill in this life. What is it? To fellowship with God. "God is faithful, by whom you were called into the fellowship of His Son" (1 Cor. 1:9).

I remember when this truth first entered my heart. I was in a time of prayer as the Lord began to speak gently to my soul. I heard Him say, "The fact that you were conceived is a testimony of your highest calling. The pinnacle of your calling is not to do a job for me. It is to share the fellowship that I share with My Son and My Spirit."

I had never considered my calling as anything beyond being a minister. I had always confined my calling to my vocation. But instead, God described my calling in terms of my relationship with Him. And as I began to journey through the Scriptures, I realized that this is, in fact, the purpose of redemption and our eternal purpose—to share intimacy with the Father and Son.

Before time began God existed and was fully satisfied in Himself. As we have already discussed, He was enjoying incredible fellowship and delight within the Godhead. From that place of enjoyment He was inspired to create humanity. And the ultimate purpose for our existence is for God to show us incredible kindness forever. Our enjoyment of Him, engaging with Him in deep intimacy, is what ultimately brings Him the greatest glory.

Ephesians 2 sheds even more light on our eternal purpose in relationship with God. It says, "And God raised us up with Christ and seated us with him in the heavenly realms in Christ Jesus" (v. 6, NIV).

Do you comprehend what God did? God has thrown open the door of unhindered fellowship that the Godhead has shared since before time began and invited us in! The entirety of creation is about this purpose: God inviting people into perfect love. You and I have the invitation to step into the fellowship the Godhead has shared, in perfection and love, forever. This is our highest purpose, our highest calling.

Jesus explained this truth by saying the same way that the Father has loved Him, He has loved us (John 15:9). He goes on to mention in John 17:23 that the Father has loved us just as He has loved Jesus.

The Father never intended for our position with Him to be lesser than that of the Son. In fact, He adopts us as His own children, welcomes us into fellowship, and then uses this amazing term: He calls us *co-heirs* with Jesus (Rom. 8:17).

When we get our identity from our vocation, we live so far below the truth of who God says we are. Oftentimes we are so aware of our fallenness and so buried under shame that we relate to God in a way that is dramatically beneath His intention. Many people picture themselves with God almost as a pet to its owner. Others may even see themselves as Jesus's bride, but they picture themselves having to approach the throne the way that Esther did, bowing in fear, hoping God will accept and welcome them.

The truth is that God has forever welcomed us into the fellowship the Godhead has shared from all eternity. We are no longer on the outside looking in. Instead, God has actually seated us in heavenly places with His Son. This seating is about our position of intimacy with God and our identity as His beloved.

Now that we comprehend that our identity and purpose are far greater than our vocation, everything should change in our approach to life. Instead of toiling for affirmation in our profession, we can live from the place of having been "accepted in the Beloved" (Eph. 1:6). When we realize we are already accepted and seated with Jesus in intimacy with the Godhead, we no longer have to strive to attain human acceptance, and we can live with a greater view of our reason for existence.

As the beloved of God, we are called to live forever in intimate partnership with deity. This is our identity and purpose forever, and it far supersedes any earthly identity or purpose we may have.

To summarize, from this lens of identity and purpose we can redefine the reasons for our careers. We have earthly jobs firstly as a declaration of God's identity as the glad worker continuously cultivating the hearts of humanity, and secondly as an invitation from God to participate with Him in His mission of seeking and saving the lost. We work because He is a worker, and we work so that we can partner with Him in His dream. Wherever He positions us to be workers, whether in ministry, an occupation, as a student, or a homemaker, each of these environs is a mission field He has called us to serve.

The switch must take place in our minds that we are not working to fulfill *our* dream and desire; we are working to participate with God in *His* dream and desire, His mission. When our paradigm shifts in this way, we are liberated to work wherever God leads, not for human accolades or status, but rather to partner with God in His plans and purposes.

As we further investigate the ideas of who God is in mission, let's take a look at God's ways as a worker. The manner of God in His service is paramount to our understanding of Him. Understanding His ways—how He goes about what He does—should transform our approach to our jobs and instruct us in the proper ways to relate to others in the marketplace or the ministry. Let's now consider who God is as a servant to gain important insight into His nature and instruct our hearts in how we are to approach the honor of serving.

CHAPTER 15

VALUES OF THE KINGDOM—SERVICE

I N EARLY 2012 I had the opportunity to spend several days with some leaders of various Chinese house churches. These leaders have been imprisoned, beaten, and suffered greatly for their faith in Jesus. They have also been instrumental in perhaps the largest revival the earth has ever seen. To this day thirty thousand people are coming to Christ daily in China! Several of the leaders I met oversee churches whose members number in the millions. Needless to say, I was humbled and honored to be able to fellowship, pray, and minister with them. They are absolutely precious men and women of God.

The outstanding characteristic of each of these individuals is that they are incredibly humble. None carry themselves in a way that makes you think they are anything more than an average person. They have none of the trappings that accompany "successful" ministry in the West—no titles, entourages, custom suits, or "rock-star" personalities. They're just brothers and sisters who dearly love Jesus.

Another characteristic that was evident about these leaders is that they serve in menial ways just as any other believer would. In the West most leaders of large ministries don't do any "meaningless" work. It might be considered below them to even carry their own bag. With these

Chinese leaders it was completely different. They had no problem clearing a table, taking out garbage, or sweeping a floor. In fact, it became evident to me that they considered it an honor to serve in this way. They were so servant-hearted that I was personally embarrassed at times when they would take my plate or give up their seat for me.

After a week of being out-served by them, things came to a crescendo. I was getting ready to depart China for Central Asia and was taken to the airport by the senior leader of a church of several million believers. I got out of the van and grabbed my fifty-pound, American "vacation-ary" suitcase. Before I could pick it up, this leader wrestled it from my hand and insisted upon carrying it for me. Earlier that week, a wheel had broken off the case, so it no longer rolled properly, meaning he would have to tote it around this huge metropolitan airport.

I protested and tried to take it back. He would not have it. "No," he motioned as he set off lugging it in front of me.

In that moment it was as if something broke inside me. This man took the position of my servant and treated me as a dignitary. This man who leads millions of believers and has suffered incredibly for Jesus considered it an honor to carry my bag. It was too much to take, and my eyes began to fill with tears. Humiliated, I yielded, schlepping behind him, humbled and broken.

Later, as I replayed that scene in my mind, the Lord began to teach me the secret these wonderful believers understand: in the kingdom privilege and honor are found in serving, not in being served. It seems so simple, but it is completely the opposite of how the world thinks and, to be honest, how many in the church think. It's normal in the West, even in ministry, for people to do what they can to work their way up the ladder of success. They build their ministries with the end in mind of becoming successful, which normally translates into having lots of parishioners and a sizable income. Of course, when a leader ascends in ministry, he is met with many opportunities such as speaking engagements, interviews, and book offers. All of this brings financial increase, and in turn people flock to be around a person who is deemed successful. The leader's persona becomes larger than life, and people swoon before them. Often they are treated like movie stars or sports idols. They have many perks and at times entire entourages just to take care of their personal needs. How different some of our big-name leaders are than the Chinese leaders!

It's noteworthy how much emphasis is placed on success strategies for church growth in the West; meanwhile the largest churches in the world are led by saints who are very simple in their approach to the gospel and life. It seems obvious that we have lost some of the keys that Jesus taught His disciples regarding the ways of the kingdom. One example is the area of serving. Who has the greater honor: the one sitting down to eat a four-course meal or the one serving those who sit at the table? Jesus used this very example (Luke 22:26–27) to explain that though the world esteems the one being served, heaven esteems the one serving. The way that heaven perceives earthly service is far different from the way the world perceives it. Whether it's in ministry or the marketplace, the kingdom value for serving is in stark opposition to the world's system.

Serving Is the Privilege

From heaven's vantage point serving—not being served—is the privilege. This fact is the key to understanding God's ways of work and service. Take a moment and meditate on Jesus's claim that He came to serve, not to be served. The *Son of God* came to serve, *not* to be served! What humility! He appeared as a humble servant, poured Himself out, and decreased until He was put to death like a murderer. His ways are decidedly not our ways.

The normal human mentality, on the other hand, is that you work your way up the ladder until you are successful, surrounded by others who clamor to serve you. The world rewards achievement and accomplishment with status and privilege. Privilege usually means that you don't have to do insignificant tasks because you are beyond that. This is exactly the opposite of the kingdom of God. In the kingdom you work your way down and decrease so that you can continually serve as many as possible. Privilege in the kingdom of God is in the serving, not in being served.

The Chinese leaders exemplified this truth, and it rocked my paradigm. What in the world was a leader of millions of people doing carrying my bag around that huge airport? He was taking the position of privilege: servanthood.

Let's consider one of the ways Jesus attempted to teach His disciples about this:

> Now there was also a dispute among them, as to which of them should be considered the greatest. And He said to them, "The kings of the Gentiles exercise lordship over them, and those who exercise authority over them are called 'benefactors.'

> But not so among you; on the contrary, he who is greatest among you, let him be as the younger, and he who governs as he who serves. For who is greater, he who sits at the table, or he who serves? Is it not he who sits at the table? Yet I am among you as the One who serves."
>
> —Luke 22:24–27

The Gentile kings Jesus refers to here loved to be called "benefactor" because it was a title that portrayed them as leaders who treated their people well. These kings were landowners who had many people who paid tributes or taxes to live in their territories.

It was well known, however, that these landowners treated the people unfairly and put heavy burdens upon them. They were, in actuality, tyrants who used their position for their own gain while demanding that the people call them by a title to depict them as kind and benevolent. Jesus said to the disciples, His key leadership team, "This is not how you are to lead. Whoever is greater among you, let him act like the younger brother."

It's understood in most cultures that the younger brother is to serve the older. Jesus says of His leaders that they should have the mentality of a younger brother, always expecting to be the servant. And then to bring clarity to what He is teaching, He says the leaders who govern are to always take the place of the servant. Jesus then emphasizes that He Himself was among them as a servant rather than as a master to model the type of leadership that His leaders are to embrace.

Servant leadership is far more than a title or nice idea. It's actually taking the lower place to serve as many as possible, even in practical and menial ways. This works for leaders in ministry and the marketplace. It also transcends roles because it is to be the normal mentality for all who are subjects of His kingdom.

Oftentimes leaders of mega-ministries think of themselves as servants because they counsel, preach, and teach regularly. While I agree that studying the Word and offering it to the congregation is serving, it is not to be the only way that leaders are to serve. When all we do is preach, we are removed from the core reality of serving. Preaching in front of crowds often has an intoxicating effect on a minister. He can begin to believe himself to be far more than he really is. If thousands of people listen to him on a regular basis, unless he is intentional about humbling himself through other forms of servanthood, he will, unbeknownst to himself, get puffed up in pride.

I talked recently to a megachurch pastor of over ten thousand people. He said, "Billy, as you speak to leaders across the country, tell them it's not about their persona and it's not about the size of their ministry. I got so caught up in the system that I lost sight of everything. I could not distinguish between who I was and who our church was. It led to me having a nervous breakdown because I was so focused on building my kingdom, I forgot about building God's kingdom."

This is exactly what Jesus was trying to keep leaders from. He was calling them to practical servanthood as a cornerstone of leadership to train them in the kingdom value of meekness. A pastor may think, "I minister so much. I really don't have time to do anything else. My service is my preaching." I would point him to Jesus. He had time to wash the disciples' feet, talk at length with the woman at the well, stoop in the dirt with the woman caught in adultery, all the while preaching and ministering daily to multitudes. Yes, I am aware in Acts 6 that the disciples said that it wasn't good for them to serve tables, and so they recruited others to do this while they devoted themselves to prayer and the ministry of the Word. Alternately, I will point out that those same disciples were trying to craft theology that explained the transition of the Testaments—a tall order for a bunch of fishermen. It wasn't until Acts 15 that they had clarity on what to do with Gentiles who were coming to faith in Christ. And that clarity came with a huge assist from Paul the apostle, the only degreed theologian of the bunch. These same disciples also supported themselves with non-ministry jobs at certain seasons, something most ministers of large congregations would never dream of. Practical servanthood can help those who are in the spotlight regularly to have their feet securely set on the ground.

As a side note, I believe the Chinese leaders lived in such humility because of one key reason: each of them has suffered for Jesus in many ways. Some had been beaten near death for their faith in Christ. All had lived in extreme poverty, and each had experienced the burden of oppression that comes with living under a Communist regime. Suffering has a way of purifying the heart and giving perspective of your own weakness. Proper perspective in turn aids humility. Their sufferings wrought in them meekness that compelled their hearts to serve.

It is from the place of humble servanthood that we connect with the heart of the Lord. He is the One who came as a servant, and we find Him when we make it our aim to serve and not to be served. As the Chinese leaders found, there is a fellowship in suffering that introduces us to Jesus's nature like nothing else. Suffering can bring us into intimacy, and servanthood is a privilege in the kingdom. In them both we find the knowledge of God and are transformed into His image.

When We Serve, We Serve the Lord

What if your pastor announced to your church that a delegation of a hundred US congressmen had contacted him and were going to visit your church to understand more deeply the vision and values of a Christian congregation? As a result, your church would have the honor of hosting and serving these leaders for a week. How would your church respond? What if the same announcement came from your pastor, but instead of congressmen it was the president with an entourage of one hundred dignitaries? Most churches would mobilize everyone they possibly could to serve. People would be stumbling all over themselves to be a part of serving these leaders.

Now let's take it up a notch. What if the same announcement came from your pastor, but it was Jesus Himself who was coming in the flesh to your church and you had the opportunity to host and serve Him? It would be "all hands on deck," and everyone would serve their hearts out.

This little example, though far-fetched, helps identify a critical truth that we have lost. Undoubtedly if Jesus showed up in the flesh at your church, everyone would participate and serve. On normal weeks, though, most churches have to work very hard to get people mobilized into ministry and service. The truth that we must rediscover is that when you serve others—the poor, the lost, your family, the church—it's every bit the same as serving Jesus directly. We must realize that it's not *as if* we are serving the Lord, but that *in reality* we are serving the Lord:

> And whatever you do, do it heartily, as to the Lord and not to men, knowing that from the Lord you will receive the reward of the inheritance; *for you serve the Lord Christ.*
> —COLOSSIANS 3:23–24, EMPHASIS ADDED

This is the key to understanding serving—whomever you serve, you are firstly serving the Lord. No wonder, then, that the privilege in the kingdom of God is in serving, not in being served, because in serving, we serve Jesus directly. This understanding will radically change our approach to service. Nothing is too small or too big. No matter what the opportunity, serving is a privilege because we get to serve Jesus in it.

Jesus's Mentality

> Yet it shall not be so among you; but whoever desires to become great among you, let him be your servant. And whoever desires to be first among you, let him be your slave—just as the Son of Man did not come to be served, but to serve, and to give His life a ransom for many.
> —MATTHEW 20:26–28

The opportunity to serve in every area of life is intentionally designed by God as a testimony of Himself. As we serve, it testifies to us of His nature and ways. In servanthood Jesus's own nature as a servant is revealed. When He came, He didn't come demanding every person to bow down to Him so that He could rule them.

When Jesus came, He came as a servant. He took a

humble job as a carpenter and lived a humble life as a man. Ultimately He served all humanity by suffering and dying the death of a thief in order to win our hearts. Paul's letter to the Philippians expresses these ideas, possibly more clearly than any passage in Scripture:

> Let this mind be in you which was also in Christ Jesus, who, being in the form of God, did not consider it robbery to be equal with God, but made Himself of no reputation, taking the form of a bondservant, and coming in the likeness of men. And being found in appearance as a man, He humbled himself and became obedient to the point of death, even the death of the cross.
> —PHILIPPIANS 2:5–8

Jesus took the place of the slave in order to show us love. He is the ultimate servant. Every opportunity we have to serve, then, is an invitation to know Jesus as the servant of all. Furthermore, Jesus's servanthood is supposed to translate into a kingdom of glad-hearted servants who joyfully lay down their lives for others, just as He laid down His life for us. In the kingdom the King is the servant; our leader has become the slave. How much more shall we take the lowest place?

This is where our paradigm must shift. In the kingdom the lowest place *is* the highest place. Privilege in the kingdom is in servanthood, not being served. Have you meditated on Jesus's humility portrayed in washing the disciples' feet?

> Jesus, knowing that the Father had given all things into His hands, and that He had come from God and was going back to God, rose from supper and

laid aside His garments, took a towel and girded Himself. After that, He poured water into the basin and began to wash the disciples' feet, and to wipe them with the towel with which He was girded. Then He came to Simon Peter. And Peter said to Him, "Lord, are You washing my feet?" Jesus answered and said to him, "What I am doing you do not understand now, but you will know after this." Peter said to Him, "You shall never wash my feet!" Jesus answered him, "If I do not wash you, you have no part with Me."

—JOHN 13:3–8

After dinner Jesus removes His robe, readies Himself with a towel and basin, and kneels down before His leadership team. On His knees, He takes each of the disciples' feet in His own hands and gently washes the filth of the day from them. Not one of them comprehended what He was modeling for them or the prophetic act He was portraying. What a picture of the cleansing of sin He would accomplish by His death on the cross just a day later! So humiliating it was for Peter that he tried to reject our Lord's service. It exposes our own arrogance when we won't allow others to serve us.

Jesus kneels. Our king stoops. Our Lord washes feet. Our King is a servant. His servanthood didn't stop at that momentous foot washing. He proceeded to the garden and came under the weight of the sin of the world, for all men, for all time. He then succumbed to arrest at the hands of the Romans, all the while serving. He endured the torture of the Roman scourge, the mockery of the crowds, and the suffering of the cross all as a servant, all for love. Finally He humbled Himself, and the author of life allowed death to overtake Him, forever becoming the servant of all.

What's more, Jesus didn't stop serving at the cross. In fact, He continues to serve us to this day, praying for us continually (Rom. 8:34). And that's not all. When Jesus returns, He will continue to show us the depths of His servant's heart:

> Blessed are those servants whom the master, when he comes, will find watching. Assuredly, I say to you that he will gird himself and have them sit down to eat, and will come and serve them.
>
> —LUKE 12:37

Jesus will serve His people at the marriage supper of the Lamb, and for all eternity we will experience the shocking humility of God in the servanthood of Christ.

Are you ready for Jesus to wash your feet? He will serve you in that day, and finally we will understand the importance of the humility of God depicted through His Son and His servant's heart toward His people. Can you imagine the pain of being served by the Son of God after having lived a life disdaining the privilege of service or, worse, having shirked every opportunity for service? How awful it would be in that day when Jesus comes to serve His people if we have lived a life longing to be served rather than to serve! Do you know Him as the servant of all? Let the revelation of Jesus, the servant of all, motivate you in every opportunity you have to serve.

The proper paradigm toward service engages our hearts with the Lord in ways not available through other means. In every act of service there is an opportunity to identify with Jesus and offer Him pure worship. Remember this the next time you are asked to do something you'd prefer to pass on to someone else. The opportunity to serve is the opportunity to find and know God. There is real privilege in the service and real intimacy with God available. A servant's heart is critical for us as we engage with Him in mission. It's through a servant's heart that we find Him and portray Him to others.

As we continue to consider who Jesus is in mission, let's turn our attention to how we are to treat others by looking at how He calls us to relate to one another. Once again we will find the knowledge of God as we consider His ways and allow them to dictate to us the proper posture for our own hearts.

CHAPTER 16

FRIENDS OF THE BRIDEGROOM

A s I SAT in the class among seventy other new staff at the International House of Prayer in Kansas City, I surveyed the room to see who else looked like a leader in the group. As I have mentioned, I had been in ministry for some years and had grown to believe I was mature in Christ. I had helped lead a ministry that had grown to over thirty-five hundred people in weekly attendance, and when the pastor was out of town, I was one of the guys who filled in for him, preaching to the congregation. I was also leading a growing and thriving youth ministry. I had come to believe that the size of my ministry was a badge of spiritual maturity. I had no idea of the arrogance of my own heart.

Being a leader can feed you with pride in a way that is indiscernible. You don't realize it, but human accolades and flattery can puff you up like a hot air balloon if you're not careful. At this time in my life I had no idea how full of pride I was and how little I knew God. Once again God was bringing me to a moment of reckoning. I was getting ready to find out how shallow my relationship with Him truly was.

As I surveyed the room, I looked for others who might be leaders like me. The room was filled with mostly eighteen- to twenty-five-year-olds who seemed to be just getting their start in the Lord. They had come to Kansas City to join the house of prayer, and most of them looked green as grass. I thought to myself that I probably didn't need to be in this training program since I was already connected with the key leaders of the ministry and this class was obviously for novices. How little I knew!

I remember the leaders of the class announcing that Gary Wiens was going to be our speaker for the morning sessions and that he would be talking about being a "friend of the Bridegroom." I recognized that the phrase was something John the Baptist had said in reference to himself, but I really didn't think it had any application today and, to be honest, I thought it was a bit of a weird topic.

Gary was a former Vineyard pastor with years of ministry experience so, though the topic seemed odd, I was interested in what he had to say. As Gary began to tell his story, I was struck with the fact that though he had been a leader in ministry for years, he confessed that he didn't really know the heart of God. I was drawn in, and the realization began to dawn on me: if this man, who was at least fifteen years my senior and had served in ministry for years as a pastor, could confess that he didn't know God, I may also be lacking in my understanding.

Gary began to explain that his paradigm of leadership had been completely wrong. The more he spoke, the more intently I listened. He explained that modern leadership teachings encouraged leaders to build their ministries by gathering people who would serve the leader and his vision. As you gather people to the vision, the ministry will grow. And so his goal had been to gather as many people as he could who would help him build his vision.

As Gary continued to talk, his pace increased and his

voice intensified from a calm conversational tone to a forceful rumble. The more he spoke, the more passionate he became. The entire message climaxed when, with a reddened face, he exclaimed, "When leaders use people to build *their ministries,* it's an abomination to God!"

At this proclamation my head spun, like a boxer reeling from a right cross.

Gary continued to thunder. "You are dealing with another Man's wife. How dare you use her for your own purposes!"

It was the knockout punch.

Everything went into slow motion as Gary's words reverberated in my head. Fear, shock, anger, and an array of emotions flooded my soul. The session ended, and I immediately ran outside to call a ministry friend. I recounted to him the things Gary said. I told him, "I've been to leadership conferences my whole life, and I've never heard anything like this. All I've ever known is gathering people to build my ministry. Gary said it's an abomination. And the worst part of it all is…I think he's right."

For several days Gary's words continued to echo in my mind: "If you use the bride to build your ministry, you are using another Man's wife."

I knew he was right.

That day my paradigm of ministry and work began to change in the light of the knowledge of God. I realized that these things are all yet another declaration of His nature. Rather than the leader being the one who gathers people to himself to fulfill his vision, the leader of any ministry or organization has the unique privilege of ministering to others as Jesus's friend. In the church we are serving Jesus's bride as His friend. In a non-ministry environment we should still relate to people in the light of God's affections for them to properly portray His heart. Let's consider some biblical pictures that portray this important truth.

Hegai the Eunuch

In the Book of Esther we have a picture of the bride and the king's servant whose job it was to serve her to make her presentable to the king. The Persian king Ahasuerus sent out messengers throughout his entire kingdom to find a suitable bride. Many young virgins were brought to the capital and entrusted to the watchful eye of Hegai, the king's eunuch. He was the custodian of the women and in charge of giving the young ladies beauty treatments to prepare them for the king. Hegai was fond of Esther, and so he gave her extra beauty treatments. When it came time for Esther to come before the king, the king desired her and chose her as queen.

Though the story of Esther is literal and speaks of real truths regarding the people of Israel, it also serves in an allegorical way to portray for us of a variety of truths, one being the heart of the king's eunuch, who is whom we represent in this story.

Just as Hegai was entrusted with overseeing the young women and looking out for their well-being, so too are ministers entrusted by God with looking out for the well-being of His bride. Just as Hegai was a eunuch, one who in no way was interested in turning the heart of the young women to himself, so too ministers are to be singularly concerned with preparing the bride for the King, in no way turning their hearts and affections after themselves. Just as Hegai's chief job was to give beauty treatments to the virgins that they would be beautified for the king, so too ministers are to give the bride "beauty treatments" through instruction in the Word, discipleship, and loving correction in order to prepare her for Jesus.

It is critical that ministers see themselves as serving the bride to prepare her for Jesus and never try to steal her affections for themselves. Far too often ministers receive the accolades of the crowd and allow themselves to become the object of the bride's affections instead of being like a "spiritual" eunuch. Ministers are never to receive the affections of the bride but are to always do whatever is necessary to point the bride toward Jesus and not themselves.

When a minister receives the affections of the bride for himself instead of seeing to it that the bride connects her heart to Jesus, he has moved from being a friend of the Bridegroom to being His enemy. Anything that is in the way of the Lord's love relationship with His people is a hindrance to love, including ministers if they steal the bride's affections. I'm not saying that the church shouldn't love her ministers. I am saying, however, there is a boundary that needs to be in place so that no man is enthroned and adored in a way that should only be reserved for the Lord. It is critical that ministers recognize their place as spiritual eunuchs tasked with serving and beautifying the bride so that she will be ready for the King, never taking her affections for himself. This is the job for all who are in leadership, whether in ministry or the marketplace, to be ones who point those we work with or lead toward Jesus.

John the Baptist

John the Baptist was the one in Scripture who first used the phrase "friend of the bridegroom." His life gives us the key example of what that phrase means. Let's consider his example.

John the Baptist was the most popular prophet in Judea since the days of Malachi. Huge crowds gathered to hear him preach and be baptized by him. Even King Herod asked for private audiences with him. While experiencing the height of "ministry momentum," the most unexpected thing happened—his ministry sphere began to diminish. Those who formerly attended his meetings were now seeking out a new prophet, Jesus. John's disciples became concerned that he was losing his influence. They saw the crowds that John had once drawn now dwindling, and so they question John about the turn of events. John's response is perhaps the most clarifying statement of what it means to be a leader in the kingdom of God:

> John answered and said, "A man can receive nothing unless it has been given to him from heaven. You yourselves bear me witness, that I said, 'I am not the Christ,' but, 'I have been sent before Him.' He who has the bride is the bridegroom; but the friend of the bridegroom, who stands and hears him, rejoices greatly because of the bridegroom's voice. Therefore this joy of mine is fulfilled. He must increase, but I must decrease."
>
> —JOHN 3:27–30

John's answer was rare for a spiritual leader in that day and even rarer for leadership in our day. He gives us a multifaceted mentality that is necessary to be a true friend of the Bridegroom.

First, he states that he had settled the issue regarding his sphere of influence. The size of his own ministry was not determined by anything or anyone other than God. If God wanted John's sphere to increase or decrease, that was up to God and not himself. If Jesus's sphere was expanding and John's was decreasing, John was completely at peace with that, resigned to the fact that no one can receive spiritual authority unless it has been granted to him from heaven. Therefore, the decrease of his own sphere in favor of the increase of Jesus's sphere was a God thing, something he was completely comfortable with.

How many leaders can say this today? How many of us are completely comfortable with God's plan for the size of our ministry, even if it means that our ministry sphere may be small compared to others? Or that it may mean that our sphere is large for a season and then much smaller for the next season? John settled it—whatever sphere of authority he received was heaven's decision, and he was comfortable with God's choice.

Often leaders fret and worry that their sphere is not what it should be. If their ministry is not large, they strive continually to increase their sphere. I agree that we should all desire to reach more people for Christ. But there is something to be said for joyfully accepting our sphere and assignment in the kingdom.

Next John the Baptist says it is right for the people to flock to Jesus because he had stated many times that he was not the Christ but simply one sent in advance to prepare the way for the Christ. At one level or another all of us are in the ministry that John describes here. None of us are the Christ, but all of us are tasked with preparing the way before the Lord. Jesus will return and receive the Father's promised inheritance of the nations. Each minister is simply an emissary sent from the Lord to prepare the way for the coming King.

Then John the Baptist explains the foundational truth that governs his ministry: Jesus is the Bridegroom, and the bride belongs to Him. John's job is simply to prepare the bride to be ready for the Bridegroom. An historic "friend of the bridegroom" was a messenger sent from the bridegroom to make the marital offer to the bride. When the would-be bride accepted, the friend of the bridegroom would see to all the marital arrangements according to the bridegroom's desires. The friend of the bridegroom was the bridegroom's servant in all matters of the wedding until the time of matrimony. John recognized his place in regard to the bride and served the Lord and the people from that place. This too should be the common paradigm for all in leadership in the kingdom.

Finally John makes it clear that he is full of joy at the fact that the Bridegroom is here. There's no greater joy than for him to see the bride's affections turning toward the Bridegroom. The commencement that he has long awaited is finally at hand. And the result will be his own decrease in the eyes of the bride while the Bridegroom becomes her every desire, the one upon whom she will place all of her affections.

How many of us in leadership can bear the thought of the decrease of our own sphere and ministries? So often the sole desire of leadership is to increase their sphere and influence without regard to what the Lord's ideas may be. Most think it's never God's idea for a ministry to decrease. However, it's clear by John's example that this is precisely what God called John to experience. What would be your response if the Lord decided the best way for you to serve the bride was by decreasing your overall numbers and budget? Would this make you full of joy?

John's example is challenging at the least and devastating at most. The more we are in the way of the bride's affections for the Bridegroom, the more we have strayed from our proper role in ministry as friends of the Bridegroom. It is required of leaders that we decrease so that He may increase.

I propose that everything, even a ministry, that exalts itself above the name of Jesus is of a different spirit than the Spirit of Christ. All that we are called to be is friends of the Bridegroom, seeing to it that the Bridegroom receives the praise and worship due Him, never taking unto ourselves the bride's devotion.

Paul Rends His Garments

The apostle Paul also powerfully modeled this mentality of leadership. He knew that his sphere was one entrusted to him by God and that his role as an apostle was to be a servant, pleasing God in all that he said and did, without regard to the praise of men (1 Thess. 2:4).

When Paul ministered in the city of Lystra, a great crowd gathered to hear the word of the Lord. As Paul was preaching the gospel, the power of the Lord was manifest to heal. Paul perceived by the Holy Spirit that a crippled man who was listening intently was full of faith. Without even touching him, Paul gave the command, "Stand up on your feet!" At his words, the cripple leapt up and walked for the entire multitude to see. Immediately, the crowd proclaimed Paul to be a god, calling him Hermes and calling Barnabas, Zeus. As the fervor of the crowd grew, they brought oxen and planned to sacrifice an offering to Paul. (See Acts 14:8–13.)

At this moment Paul had a decision to make. Would he allow the people to enthrone him, or would he do everything in his power to take none of their affections for himself? Too often in our day, when ministers are faced with this same decision, while they tell the crowd to give glory to God, they in fact receive the devotion of the crowd for themselves. They in fact use the ministry as a means for profiting and in doing so take part of the glory due the Lord unto themselves. I'm not saying a laborer is not worthy of his wage, but where did we get the idea that a minister with a large congregation should be compensated in the same way as a CEO of a major corporation? Could it be that we've allowed the people to sacrifice to us instead of preventing them?

Look at Paul's example and ask the Lord to check your own heart:

> But when the apostles Barnabas and Paul heard of this, they tore their clothes and ran in among the multitude, crying and saying, "Men, why are you doing these things? We also are men with the same nature as you..."
>
> —ACTS 14:14–15

When faced with being enthroned as gods by the people, Paul chose the route of a friend of the Bridegroom, even if it meant humiliating himself in front of the masses. One minute, at his command, the lame is leaping, completely healed of a lifelong infirmity. The next moment Paul is tearing his shirt off so that the people would recognize he is only a man, no different from them. A friend of the Bridegroom lives by this mentality: when the worship of the people is directed toward them and not the Lord, they humble themselves before the people to exalt Jesus.

In this case it cost Paul dearly. Not only did he humble himself before the people, but these exact same people who were exalting him as a god were poisoned against him a few days later by the Jewish leaders from Antioch. The crowd that wanted to sacrifice to him now drug him out of the city and stoned him, leaving him for dead.

There may be a human price to pay by choosing to humble yourself before people. They may not give you the accolades they once did—or, worse, they may disrespect you, even to the point of assassinating your character. But what's worse—receiving man's praise and becoming an obstacle to intimacy between the bride and the Bridegroom, or decreasing in the eyes of the people that Jesus may receive the worship that is due Him? No humiliation in the eyes of men is worse than being exalted by men to the point that Jesus is not given all the glory. This is what Paul and John the Baptist understood; to be a friend of the Bridegroom, He must increase, and we must decrease.

Being a friend of the Bridegroom is a critical concept for each of us as workers, leaders, or ministers. The position of our hearts as we relate to others must be to serve them by introducing them to Jesus the Bridegroom, never allowing our own persona to be exalted in any way.

This mentality offers us a different approach to our jobs and ministries. With this paradigm we will have a different motive for all that we do in mission: to draw everyone's attention to Jesus. Humanism always seeks to point to people as the object of accolades and praise. But a friend of the Bridegroom will see to it that any praise that is pointed his direction will in turn be offered to Jesus, the only One who is worthy of human adoration.

Once again the knowledge of God as a Bridegroom directs us in how we go about our lives in this institution of mission. When we see Him as He is and honor Him rightly, we will do all within our power to connect hearts to Him and nothing else—especially not ourselves. Our partnership with God in His mission is expressed when we recognize ourselves as a friend of the Bridegroom and we serve Him and His bride by decreasing that He may be exalted.

CONCLUSION

F ROM OUR RELATIONSHIPS and our jobs to money and our mission, all of the institutions of life are divinely designed with one chief end in mind: to declare the knowledge of God. He has set up the entire construct of creation to continually reveal Himself. We live in a maze built by God, in which He has written His name on every wall. He has hidden details of His nature just beneath the surface in every one of life's key institutions. When we take the time to step back and consider who God is in each area of our lives, we encounter Him in a most remarkable way. On the other hand, when we approach life with a human-centered focus, we miss the most important point about life: God.

Life is all about knowing Him. Through parenting we find the Father, through marriage we discover the Bridegroom, through our jobs we meet the Servant, and through money we're introduced to the Steward. Through encountering God in each of life's institutions, we find a critical truth: our ability to do anything well in life is directly related to knowing God. Transformation never comes solely through human means. It comes through revelation. Knowing God in our marriages is what makes a great marriage. Knowing God in our jobs is what makes a great career. Knowing God is what makes a great life— not an easy life, but a full life, an abundant life.

It's only through knowing God in life's institutions that we are able to rightly view them and do them. Ancient astronomers believed that the entire universe orbited around the earth—that we were the center. A similar error is made by masses daily who act as if we are the centerpiece of all that exists. If we believe that life is primarily about us, that we are somehow "the center of the universe," we will never truly come to know the One who has woven together the very framework of creation.

Without the knowledge of Him, we lack the character of Christ. The formation of Christ in our hearts is a by-product of the revelation of God filling our souls. In Christ we become partakers of the divine nature through the knowledge of Him. And through the knowledge of Him we thrive. When we perceive Him, we soar. When we see Him, we truly live. Through the knowledge of God we are transformed. And this is where success is ultimately found—not in being a better you, but in being conformed to the image of Jesus.

So what's the application? What's the takeaway? God. He is the application. The knowledge of Him is success. We have languished far too long with our eyes on ourselves operating from a human center, looking for measurable results. We've set our bar far too low, when the One who is immeasurable should be our quest. He is the center. He is our reason. He is what life is about. Knowing God is our purpose, and everything else is just details. Partnership with the divine is our mission, and all other pursuits are merely side attractions.

Through the knowledge of Him we find our purpose. Whatever you do in life, it is to be a result of connecting with Him in His mission. It's only through joining God's plan that the pursuits of our lives make sense. And it's only through engaging in His mission that we can scratch the itch in our soul to make an impact.

Everyone has a desire for accomplishment and

achievement, a desire to leave a legacy. Real impact is only made through finding God and revealing Him to others. Your calling is far greater than any earthly title; your calling is to partner with the One who is uncreated.

Living life through these lenses requires persistent pursuit of God. Understanding and knowing God doesn't come cheaply. But God is ever willing to reveal Himself to anyone who searches Him out. Just like coming to know a new friend intimately, we must approach our relationship with God the same way. Relationships are built over time through communication and shared experiences. Our relationship with God is no different. The requirement of prayer to perceive and know Him cannot be overstated. It's through communion with Him that we begin to comprehend His ways. We must slow down and unplug from the volume of distractions that have left us dull in our knowledge of Him and approach Him anew with hearts hungry for encounter. Communication is key, and so the journey into the knowledge of Him is a journey into prayer.

This is no quick trip. It's not a five-minute errand; it's a fifty-year voyage.

I encourage you to start by setting a five-year goal to know God more. Begin with an attainable daily plan to spend time with Him in prayer and study of the Word. Attainable is key. There's no reason to bite off more than you can chew with your schedule; you've already bitten of more than you can chew by seeking God. Do what you can. For some, starting with a focused thirty minutes a day is a stretch. For others, you need to plan for two hours, minimum. Whatever your plan, approach Him daily with a heart open to perceive and know Him. Ask Him to reveal Himself to you. Query Him on what He is like and what He likes. Pursue knowing His heart and His emotions, and practice your plan over the long haul. Make it attainable so you can do it for five years. Jump in and go for it, and don't even assess your progress until the five years is up.

If you miss a day here or there, no worries. You're on a five-year course. The key is consistency over time—seeking God diligently over years. We don't study Him like cramming for a test in school. We engage with Him like running a marathon. Diligence with zeal is carried out through a long-term commitment of consistent faithfulness. Go for it. And in doing so, you will find transformation.

It's the slow burn, the slow cooker, the Crock-Pot, not the microwave. Most people want an explosion, but explosions last only a moment. What they really need is the subtle ignition of a fuse, which will ultimately lead to a monumental detonation of revelation in the knowledge of Him.

This is the end of our brief journey into the knowledge of God, but I pray it's only the beginning of your lifelong quest. The knowledge of God is a worthy pursuit. Jesus described it as the only necessary thing. I pray you will seek Him out and that as you come to know Him, you will be a beacon of light to others who look for Him. Few have embraced the journey, but all who have are known for it. If a man knows God, the same is known of him. I pray this becomes your story. Make Him your purpose, your pursuit, your hobby, and your leisure. In finding Him, you will find what we're here for: to know Him.

RECOMMENDED READING

Charnock, Stephen. *The Existence and Attributes of God.* Grand Rapids, MI: Baker Books, 1996.

Packer, J. I. *Knowing God.* Downers Grove, IL: InterVarsity Press, 1993.

Pink, A. W. *The Attributes of God.* Grand Rapids, MI: Baker Books, 2006.

Tozer, A. W. *The Knowledge of the Holy.* New York: HarperCollins, 1978.

Tozer, A. W. *The Attributes of God*, vol. 1 and 2. Camp Hill, PA: Wingspread Publishers, 2007.

NOTES

Chapter 1
Who Are You, Lord?

1. Brother Lawrence, *The Practice of the Presence of God* (Castle Rock, CO: Perieco, 2009), 78.

Chapter 2
The Knowledge of God

1. J. I. Packer, *Knowing God* (London: Hodder and Stoughton, 1973), 39.
2. A. W. Tozer, *The Knowledge of the Holy* (New York: HarperCollins, 1961), 3–4.

Chapter 3
His Greatness Is Unsearchable

1. A. W. Pink, "The Fear of the Lord Is the Beginning of Wisdom," http://www.sermonindex.net/modules/articles/index .php?view=article&aid=720? (accessed February 7, 2013).
2. Tozer, *The Knowledge of the Holy*, vii.
3. NASA.gov, "Go to the Head of the Solar System," http:// www.nasa.gov/audience/forkids/kidsclub/text/games/levelfive/ KC_Solar_System.html#Answers (accessed February 7, 2013).
4. Sapce.com, "How Big Is the Sun? | Size of the Sun," http://www.space.com/17001-how-big-is-the-sun-size-of-the -sun.html (accessed February 7, 2013).
5. National Geographic Education, "Equator," http:// education.nationalgeographic.com/education/encyclopedia/ equator/?ar_a=1 (accessed February 7, 2013).
6. National Geographic, "Sun," http://science .nationalgeographic.com/science/space/solar-system/sun-article/ (accessed February 7, 2013).
7. National Geographic Education, "Earth," http://education .nationalgeographic.com/education/encyclopedia/earth/?ar_a=1 (accessed February 7, 2013).

8. NASA.gov, "What Is Pluto?", http://www.nasa.gov/audience/forstudents/k-4/stories/what-is-pluto-k4.html (accessed February 7, 2013).

9. NASA.gov, "What Does the Edge of the Solar System Look Like?", http://www.nasa.gov/vision/universe/solarsystem/voyager_heliosphere.html (accessed February 7, 2013).

10. National Geographic, "Billions of Earthlike Planets Crowd Milky Way?", Daily News, http://news.nationalgeographic.com/news/billions-of-earthlike-planets-found-in-milky-way/ (accessed February 7, 2013).

11. National Geographic, "Galaxies," http://science.nationalgeographic.com/science/space/universe/galaxies-article/ (accessed February 7, 2013).

12. National Geographic, "Billions of Earthlike Planets Crowd Milky Way?"

13. Wiki.answers.com, "How Many Solar System in the Universes are There?", http://wiki.answers.com/Q/How_many_solar_system_in_the_universes_are_there (accessed February 7, 2013).

14. Quotes Daddy, http://www.quotesdaddy.com/quote/1392075/thomas-watson/gods-center-is-everywhere-his-circumference-nowhere (accessed February 7, 2013).

15. Tozer, *The Knowledge of the Holy*, 8.

Chapter 4
Life's Journey Into the Knowledge of God

1. Richard Foster, *Prayer: Finding the Heart's True Home* (New York: HarperOne, 1992), 171.

2. Packer, *Knowing God*, 34.

Chapter 5
Who Is God in Marriage?

1. Mike Mason, *Mystery of Marriage* (Colorado Springs, CO: Multnomah Books), 103.

2. BirdWatchersDigest.com, "20 Things You (Probably) Don't Know About Birds," http://www.birdwatchersdigest.com/bwdsite/solve/faqs/20things.php (accessed February 8, 2013).

3. Ibid.

4. Don E. Wilson and F. Russell Cole, *Common Names of Mammals of the World* (Washington DC: Smithsonian Institution Scholarly Press, 2000).

Chapter 6
The Bridegroom's Passion

1. New Advent, "Betrothal," http://www.newadvent.org/cathen/02537c.htm (accessed March 6, 2013).
2. *Merriam-Webster's Collegiate Dictionary*, 11th edition (Springfield, MA: Merriam-Webster, Inc., 2003), s.v. "ravish."

Chapter 10
The Father's Delight in the Son

1. Blue Letter Bible, "Dictionary and Word Search for *sachaq* (Strong's 7832)," http://www.blueletterbible.org/lang/lexicon/lexicon.cfm?Strongs=H7832&t=KJV (accessed February 8, 2013).

Chapter 12
Who Is God in Finances?

1. As quoted in Rick Warren, *The Purpose-Drive Life* (Grand Rapids, MI: Zondervan, 2002), 40. Viewed at Google Books online.

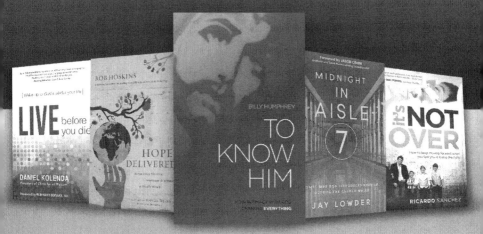

FREE NEWSLETTERS
TO HELP EMPOWER YOUR LIFE

Why subscribe today?

❏ **DELIVERED DIRECTLY TO YOU.** All you have to do is open your inbox and read.

❏ **EXCLUSIVE CONTENT.** We cover the news overlooked by the mainstream press.

❏ **STAY CURRENT.** Find the latest court rulings, revivals, and cultural trends.

❏ **UPDATE OTHERS.** Easy to forward to friends and family with the click of your mouse.

CHOOSE THE E-NEWSLETTER THAT INTERESTS YOU MOST:

- Christian news
- Daily devotionals
- Spiritual empowerment
- And much, much more

SIGN UP AT: **http://freenewsletters.charismamag.com**

8178

Made in the USA
Middletown, DE
11 August 2017